Essential
Moscow and St Petersburg

by

CHRISTOPHER AND MELANIE RICE

Christopher Rice writes regularly on Russian and
Soviet affairs and holds a PhD from the Centre for
Russian and East European Studies at Birmingham
University. His wife Melanie is also a writer and has
shared his fascination with Moscow and St Petersburg
ever since their first joint visit in 1978.

D1324971

AA

Produced by AA Publishing

Written by Christopher and
Melanie Rice
Peace and Quiet section
by Paul Sterry

Revised second edition January 1996
First published 1991

Edited, designed and produced by
AA Publishing. © The Automobile
Association 1996. Maps © The
Automobile Association 1996.

Distributed in the United Kingdom by
AA Publishing, Norfolk House,
Priestley Road, Basingstoke,
Hampshire, RG24 9NY.

A CIP catalogue record for this book
is available from the British Library.

ISBN 0 7495 1168 0

The contents of this publication are
believed correct at the time of
printing. Nevertheless, the
publishers cannot be held
responsible for any errors or
omissions or for changes in the
details given in this guide or for the
consequences of any reliance on the
information provided by the same.
Assessments of attractions, hotels,
restaurants and so forth are based
upon the author's own experience
and, therefore, descriptions given in
this guide necessarily contain an
element of subjective opinion which
may not reflect the publisher's
opinion or dictate a reader's own
experience on another occasion.

**We have tried to ensure accuracy
in this guide, but things do change
and we would be grateful if
readers would advise us of any
inaccuracies they may encounter.**

Published by AA Publishing, a
trading name of Automobile
Association Developments Limited,
whose registered office is Norfolk
House, Priestley Road, Basingstoke,
Hampshire, RG24 9NY.

Registered number 1878835.
Colour separation: BTB Colour
Reproduction Ltd, Whitchurch,
Hampshire

Printed by: Printers S.R.L.,Trento,
Italy

*Front cover picture: Novodevichiy
Convent, Smolensk Cathedral,
Moscow*

Contents

This book employs a simple rating system to help choose which places to visit:

✓	'top ten'

◆◆◆ do not miss
◆◆ see if you can
◆ worth seeing if you have time

Russia's capital and a prime tourist attraction: Moscow

INTRODUCTION

We still call it Russia but officially it is the Russian Federation, comprising Russia itself and 17 autonomous republics. Russia is the largest country in the world, stretching nearly 9,000 miles (15,000km) from east to west, crossing 11 time zones and covering an area of 6,593,391 square miles (17,076,804sq km), more than 70 times that of the United Kingdom. The population is approximately 140 million, concentrated in the area west of the Ural mountains. The capital of the Russian Federation is Moscow. With a population of 9 million, Moscow is not only the largest city in Russia but also one of the great capitals of Europe and a thriving commercial, industrial and communications centre. St Petersburg, with nearly 5 million inhabitants, is Russia's second city. For more than 200 years, from 1703 to 1918, it was the capital, first as

St Petersburg, then, during the First World War, as Petrograd. After the death of Lenin in 1924, it was renamed Leningrad but reverted to its original name in 1991. It remains an important seaport and industrial centre, but visitors are attracted to it for its rich architectural and artistic heritage and its vibrant cultural life. For sheer beauty St Petersburg has few equals.

Moscow, Russia's Soul

Think of Russia and the chances are you think of the Kremlin with its great fortress walls, gleaming cupolas and ornate palaces. For centuries this was a place of refuge, from the ravages of cruel Tatar hordes, from the excesses of tyrannical serf-owners, from the spectre of poverty and hunger. Today it is the seat of government of one of the world's most influential states, as well as the country's premier tourist attraction. Beyond the Kremlin is a city full of architectural monuments and fascinating places of interest: Red Square – the garish St Basil's Cathedral contrasting with the sombre Lenin mausoleum; the elegant Bolshoi Theatre; charming Arbat, with its street musicians and pavement artists; the Tretyakov Gallery, overflowing with artistic treasures. You can shop on the fashionable Tverskaya Ulitsa or in the GUM shopping mall; explore the luxurious and amazingly efficient metro system; travel back in time by visiting some of the city's ancient churches and monasteries, many restored for worship. You can attend a rock concert in Gorky Park (Park im A M Gorkovo), watch a football match, or go for a swim at Silver Pine Forest (Serebryanniy Bor). You can eat in any number of the city's loud and colourful restaurants, or take a night out at the world famous State Circus. Whatever your taste, there is something in Moscow for you.

St Petersburg, Window on the West

St Petersburg is an artificial creation, the brainchild of one man; the modernising tsar, Peter the Great. Turning his back on Moscow, which he despised as primitive and backward-looking, Peter chose a site on the shores of the Baltic and transformed an unpromising landscape of islands and marshland into one of

INTRODUCTION

Buskers in Arbat Street, Moscow, a magnet for artists, poets and musicians

the world's most beautiful cities. He called it Sankt Petersburg. Now, nearly 300 years later, St Petersburg is a thriving metropolis; but it is also a unique architectural monument – a dazzling ensemble of palaces and cathedrals, rivers and canals, grandiose squares and sweeping perspectives, a succession of beautiful pinks, greens, blues and yellows. For the art lover, St Petersburg, with its 50 museums and art galleries, is a paradise. The Hermitage alone boasts magnificent works by Raphael and da Vinci, Rembrandt and Rubens, Cézanne and van Gogh, Picasso and Matisse. Or, if your interests are historical, you can journey back into the city's past with a visit to the beautiful but forbidding Peter-Paul Fortress. St Petersburg is also the cradle of the revolution, and you can still see the Kseshinskaya Mansion (Osobnyak Kshesinskoy), where Lenin had an office in 1917, and the Smolniy Institute, from which the Bolsheviks organised the seizure of power. St Petersburg has always been at the forefront of the nation's cultural development. Pushkin and

Dostoyevsky once walked these streets; so, too, did Tchaikovsky and Rachmaninov, Pavlova and Nijinsky. Today you can enjoy the best of the city's opera and ballet by spending an evening at the Mariinskiy Theatre (Mariinskiy Teatr), formerly known as the Kirov, or by attending a concert at the Philharmonic Hall, named after another distinguished Petersburger, Dimitry Shostakovitch.

It is pretty likely that, at some point in your stay, you will want to go shopping on the famous Nevskiy Prospekt, stopping off at Yeliseev's food store, perhaps, or the Gostiniy Dvor. In the summer you can stroll through the city's many parks and gardens or take a boat trip on the Neva. Out of town there are the palaces of Tsarskoe Selo, Peterhof and Pavlovsk to wonder at, so you will never be at a loss for things to do.

Weather

Both Moscow and St Petersburg are year-round destinations. The winters are cold, but invigorating, with frequent snow showers and sparkling frosts. Summers have a reasonable amount of sunshine and the odd sweltering day but, bring a raincoat!

If you are lucky enough to visit St Petersburg in mid-July you will be able to sample the famous White Nights, when darkness lasts all of 40 minutes and night and day are barely distinguishable.

Russia's changing face

In August 1991 conservative plotters opposed to Soviet president, Mikhail Gorbachev staged a *coup* while he was holidaying in the Crimea. The *coup* was a fiasco but its consequences were profound: nothing less than the banning of the Communist Party, which had ruled unopposed for more than 70 years and, shortly afterwards, the disintegration of the Soviet Union itself. The chief beneficiary of the political earthquake was Boris Yeltsin who was elected President of the new Russian Federation.

Only two years later Yeltsin's erstwhile supporters, critical of the pace of reform and of the perceived failure of the president to address the economic crisis, staged a second *coup*, which resulted in Yeltsin laying siege to his own parliament. Again the president emerged victorious, but this time at a price – in the ensuing parliamentary elections (December 1993) the right, led by the eccentric Russian chauvinist, Vladimir Zhirinovsky, captured nearly a quarter of the total vote.

Since that time the lower house of parliament, known as the State Duma, has been locked in almost continuous combat with the president who still hopes to win a second term against all the odds in 1996. He will need to convince an increasingly cynical public that the country has not polarised into a society of haves and have-nots, that the forces of law and order still remain in control and that market reforms are more than a stepping stone to riches for criminals and opportunists.

MOSCOW

BACKGROUND

Set back opposite City Hall (Moskovskiy Soviet) on Tverskaya Ulitsa, one of Moscow's main thoroughfares, is a statue of a warrior on horseback, arm outstretched in command. This is Yuriy Dolgoruky (George the long-armed), commonly regarded as the founder of Moscow. In 1147 Prince Yuriy of Suzdal invited a neighbouring prince from Novgorod to a banquet with the words 'Come to me, brother, in Moscow'. In fact, there had already been a settlement here for some time, but not a very important one. Moscow was just one of a number of military outposts in the northern principality of Vladimir-Suzdal, which had been gaining in importance since the decline and fragmentation of the once powerful Kievan state. In Yury's time there were only a few houses and a hunting lodge, and, by 1156, a small wooden fortress or *kreml* (Kremlin), situated near the present Borovitsky Tower at the confluence of the Moskva (Moscow) and Neglinnaya rivers.

Two namesakes merge: Moskva – Moscow city – reflected in the Moskva River

Gold covers the roof of the Kremlin's Cathedral of the Annunciation, a private place of worship and a public display of wealth

The Mongols

Moscow's importance grew out of national catastrophe. In 1237 Batu, grandson of Genghis Khan, unleashed his ferocious Mongol hordes on Russia, crossing the Volga with lightning speed and laying waste everything before him. The following year, Moscow was burnt to the ground and its inhabitants massacred. After Kiev was captured and sacked in 1240, Batu Khan established his capital at Saray on the Volga and all Russia's princes had to appear there to have their titles confirmed. They became tax collectors for their Mongol overlords but were allowed considerable independence within the confines of their territories. The rulers of Moscow exploited this situation to the full, winning the confidence of their conquerors by carrying out their wishes assiduously. In 1276 Prince Daniel, son of the great warrior, Alexander Nevskiy, made Moscow his permanent capital and strengthened its defences by building the

Danilovskiy Monastery, the first of a series of
fortified monasteries around the periphery of
the town, named in this case after his own
patron saint. His successor, Ivan 1, became the
first Grand Prince of Moscow in 1328, a reward
for his efficiency as a tax collector (he was
known to his people as Kalita, or 'money bag').

Medieval Moscow

Moscow's prestige was further enhanced when
the head of the Orthodox Church, Metropolitan
Peter, transferred the Holy See here from
Vladimir. The town grew quickly in size and
importance. Commanding the trade routes
along the Oka and Volga Rivers, as well as
overland routes from Central Europe, Moscow
drew merchants and commercial travellers like
a magnet. Dealers in fish, furs, hides and cloth
all made their way here, while the labour force
was swelled by fugitives from less politically
stable regions. Noblemen and their retainers,
members of the clergy and soldiers with their
dependants together made up the remainder
of the rapidly growing population. As the grip
of the Mongol occupation began to ease,
towards the end of the 14th century, Moscow
grew in military might and confidence. In 1380,
Grand Prince Dimitry, having received the
blessing of St Sergius, founder of the great
monastery of Sergievo Posad, inflicted the first
defeat on the Tatars at the Battle of Kulikovo on
the Don (from which the prince became known
as Dimitry Donskoi). This celebrated victory
was far from marking the end of Mongol rule –
Moscow was burned to the ground in
retaliation only two years later – but it was a
step towards liberation and a powerful hint of
what was to come.
When Ivan III came to the throne in 1462, he
inherited territories eight times greater than a
century before. But he was not one to sit on his
laurels: by the time he died in 1505 Muscovy
was the largest state in Europe, with an area of
nearly 500,000 square miles (1,300,000sq km).
Yaroslavl, Rostov, Tver and Novgorod, once
independent princedoms, were swallowed up
by their insatiable neighbour. Ivan's writ ran
from the Ural mountains to the Arctic Sea. At
the same time, he strengthened his dynastic

position by marrying Sophia, or Zoë, niece of the last Emperor of Constantinople. The two-headed eagle of Byzantium now became the emblem of the rulers of Russia, and Ivan began to use the title Tsar (Caesar). When Constantinople fell to the Turks in 1453, he went a step further, declaring Moscow the third Rome, the new centre of the Orthodox Church. His authority was now absolute, as he revealed in 1480 when he ceased paying tribute to the Khan.

Italian Influences

Ivan now turned his attention to the Kremlin and embarked on an ambitious building programme. The cathedrals dating from the time of Dimitry Donskoi were replaced, as foreign architects and craftsmen, mainly from Northern Italy, arrived to supplement the home-grown talent from Pskov, Vladimir and Novgorod. The result was a unique blend of the Renaissance and the East. The Cathedrals of the Annunciation, the Dormition and the Archangel Michael all appeared in the space of little more than twenty years, to be joined by a magnificent new palace, the Palace of the Facets, as it is now called. Meanwhile, the white limestone walls and towers of the Kremlin were pulled down to make way for the present battlements and watchtowers of red brick.

A New Prosperity

Although Moscow remained vulnerable to Tatar attack (the city was captured and burned to the ground in 1571), it continued to grow in size and prosperity. An English visitor, Giles Fletcher, thought it bigger than London, and there were reckoned to be more than 40,000 houses. The heart of the city, then as now, was the Kremlin, surrounded on three sides by a moat, fed by the Neglinnaya Stream. Red Square, immediately beyond the Kremlin moat, was a bustling market place; here, too, important announcements were made and executions carried out. There was another trading quarter immediately behind what is now the GUM shopping mall, stretching as far as Lubyanka Square. This area, known as the Kitai-gorod, was surrounded by another stone wall and there were additional wooden fortifications further out, roughly between the present Boulevard and Garden Rings. There was a large population of labourers and craftsmen, many employed by the Court. The provisions department alone employed more than 150 cooks, water carriers, dishwashers and food inspectors while the court stables provided work for an additional 300 servants. Many of the tsar's employees lived in a suburb still known today as the Arbat, where the street names (Old Stables Lane, Silver Lane, Carpenters Lane) commemorate the various trades. Another artisan quarter is centred on the present Taganka Square (Taganskaya Ploshchad), whose name derives from the kettles used by the tsar's soldiers during their campaigns against the Tatars. There was a settlement of potters here too, while the royal weavers lived further out, at Khamovniki. The Church of St Nicholas in Khamovniki (Tserkov Nikolv v Khamovnikakh) is still known as the

Russian and Italian architecture are blended in the Cathedral of the Assumption, or the Dormition, a five-domed Kremlin church

Weavers' Church. The skyline of 16th-century Moscow was punctuated with gilded onion domes and bell towers, for there were over 200 churches and 18 religious houses, including the Danilovskiy, Don and Andronikov monasteries, which guarded the southern and eastern approaches to the city.

The Time of Troubles

That Moscow continued to flourish during this period is remarkable, given the political turbulence which marked the latter part of the century. The trouble began in the reign of Ivan the Terrible (1533–84). The first ruler of Moscow to be crowned Tsar, his reign had begun with a number of military successes, the most important of which was the capture of Kazan, which prompted the building of St Basil's Cathedral in Red Square. During the 1560s, however, Ivan turned on the *boyars* (noblemen) who had marred his minority, and his attacks soon degenerated into an irrational and generalised persecution. Gangs of thugs called *oprichniki,* wearing a distinctive black uniform and the badge of a severed dog's head and broom, terrorised the population. Ivan's vicious spells were punctuated with periods of tearful remorse, in which he sent lists of his victims to monasteries so that the monks might pray for them. His obsession with domestic intrigue was such that he became oblivious to the external threat. His Muscovite subjects suffered the consequences when the Tatars captured and sacked the city in 1571. Worse was to come. The period following Ivan's death in 1584 is known to historians as the Time of Troubles. The feeble Tsar Fyodor was replaced in 1598 by Boris Godunov, who was challenged by a pretender claiming to be Ivan the Terrible's youngest son, Dimitry. A second 'False Dimitry' emerged after Boris' death in 1605 and received military help from the Poles, who occupied Moscow in 1610. Two years later they were ousted by patriotic forces under the leadership of Kuzma Minin, a butcher from Nizhny-Novgorod, and Prince Dimitry Pozharskiy. (A statue to both was later erected in Red Square, near St Basil's Cathedral.) The chaos finally ended in 1613 with the election of

The colourful Church of St Nicholas, known as the Weavers' Church after the royal weavers who once lived in the area

Tsar Mikhail Romanov, founder of the dynasty which was to survive until the revolution.

The 17th century saw the continued expansion of the Russian Empire. Part of the Ukraine as far as the River Dnieper (and including the city of Kiev) was acquired in 1667 and the colonisation of Siberia went on apace. By 1700 Russian settlers had reached Okhotsk on the Pacific coast, and clashed for the first time with the Chinese on the Amur River.

The Russians did not have it all their own way. In 1669 the Don cossacks, led by Stenka Razin, launched a rebellion which took government forces almost two years to quell. In June 1671 Razin was finally captured, brought to Moscow and drawn and quartered in Red Square: Ulitsa Varvarka, between St Basil's and the Rossiya Hotel, marks the route of his last journey.

BACKGROUND – MOSCOW

Moscow Neglected

During the reign of Peter the Great (1682–1725) Russia's attention shifted northwards toward the Baltic, with damaging consequences for Moscow. The new city of St Petersburg was officially declared the capital in 1712, two years before another decree forbade building in stone in any other city. Ironically, Peter's obsession with Westernisation can be traced back to his youth in Moscow, when he was irresistibly drawn to the Foreigner's Quarter (Nemetskaya Sloboda), near the modern Kursk Railway Station (Kurskiy Vokzal). The two regiments of which he was most proud, the Preobrazhensky and Semyonovsky Guards, were also named after Moscow villages. Moscow was not wholly eclipsed by the new northern capital. During Peter's reign the nobility were compelled to live in St Petersburg, but after his death there was a wholesale exodus south from its bleak and inhospitable shores. A period of concentrated building followed. Fine new mansions and town houses, built originally in wood and later in stone, began to transform the Arbat and Prechistenka districts into 'nests of the gentry'. The fabulously wealthy Sheremetiev family used

Moscow's Lomonsov University, built in the imposing Gothic style favoured by Stalin

serf labour to develop their out-of-town estates at Ostankino, near the All Russian Exhibition Centre or Tekhnopark (VDNKh), and Kuskovo, while the Golitsyns and Yussupovs followed suit at Arkhangelskoye. New thoroughfares, like the Tverskaya, were opened up, two large hospitals were built and Russia's first university founded just across from the Alexander Garden in 1775. One project, fortunately, was not realised. This was Catherine the Great's plan for a huge new classical palace to replace the Kremlin. In the end only the architect's model was completed, though a number of important buildings were demolished to clear the site.

War and Peace

Napoleon's grim sojourn in Moscow is brilliantly described in Tolstoy's *War and Peace*. The hut where Kutuzov and the other Russian generals deliberated on the eve of his entry has been preserved in a building on Kutuzovskiy Prospekt. When the French were compelled to evacuate the city, Napoleon gave orders for the Kremlin, the Novodevichiy Convent and other important buildings to be blown up, but Russian troops arrived just in time to prevent this disaster. They were unable, however, to do anything about the great fire which started mysteriously and is said to have consumed more than 80 per cent of Moscow's predominantly wooden houses. Reconstruction, mainly in brick, began immediately, and some of the city's finest buildings and squares date from this period. The Manège, formerly a military riding school and now an exhibition centre, was completed to a French design in 1825. Theatre Square, with its magnificent centrepiece, the Bolshoi Theatre, dates from the same period, as does the Alexander Garden, laid out over the fetid Neglinnaya stream in 1821. New thoroughfares like Prechistenka were planned and adorned with Empire-style mansions.

Moscow Transformed

Much more dramatic changes occurred during the second half of the century as Moscow responded to the government's twin goals of modernisation and industrialisation. The city

BACKGROUND – MOSCOW

The palatial underground railway in Moscow gives a grandiose touch to commuting

was a vibrant financial and commercial centre and, with its nine railway stations, the hub of Russia's communications network. The population of 350,000 in 1840 increased to just over a million in 1900, making Moscow the 10th largest city in the world. By this time, two-thirds of the inhabitants (mostly peasants from the surrounding countryside) lived outside the city proper in poorly lit and ill-paved factory 'suburbs' – little shanty towns separated by acres of neglected wasteland. But factories and workshops invaded the central districts, too, their belching chimneys casting a grimy pall over once resplendent buildings. There were a number of 'no go' areas, like the Khitrov market near the Rossiya Hotel and a notorious red light district, northeast of the Bolshoi Theatre. Yet there were still country lanes twisting through the Arbat, complete with grassy courtyards, kitchen gardens, stables, even cocks and hens. Not for nothing was Moscow known as the 'big village'. There were plenty of pleasant green spaces outside the city too, Sokolniki Park, for example, or Sparrow Hills.

Revolution and Civil War

Fierce fighting took place in Moscow during the Revolution of 1905, when workers and revolutionaries set up barricades in the Presnya district. In November 1917 the Bolshevik seizure of power was more violent here than in St Petersburg, with shooting in Red Square and around the Arbat, and running battles between workers and troops. Lenin moved the capital back to Moscow in March 1918 and stayed for a few days in the National Hotel, before taking up residence in the Kremlin. During the ensuing Civil War, the city was plunged into anarchy and Lenin himself was held up by armed bandits while on a drive through the suburbs, early in 1919.

Stalin's Imprint

Stalin's Plan for the Reconstruction of Moscow envisaged cutting a swathe through several of the old districts and demolishing countless buildings of historical interest. The widened Gorky Street (Ulitsa Tverskaya), Leninskiy Prospekt and Prospekt Mira all date from this period, as does the lavish Metro system. In October 1941 the government evacuated Moscow in the face of the Nazi advance, but the invading forces were driven back from the outskirts of the city in what was one of the major turning points of the war.

Moscow Today

The postwar period has been one of continued, planned expansion, with suburbs relentlessly pushing out the frontiers of the city. The result is a rather soulless panorama of identical tower blocks. There have been comparatively few changes in the city centre. Stalin's famous 'wedding cake' buildings (the University at Sparrow Hills and the Ministry of Foreign Affairs, for example) date from the 1940s and 1950s, while the new Kalinin Prospekt is a '60s development. More heartening than these Brave New World efforts has been the recent emphasis on restoration and preservation, the best examples being the National and Metropole (Metropol) Hotels. The sight of Western shop fronts, such as Estée Lauder on Tverskaya Ulitsa, is no longer a novelty.

WHAT TO SEE – MOSCOW (MOSKVA)

Western visitors often come away disappointed from Russian museums, not because the exhibits are uninteresting, but because of the unimaginative presentation. That said, there are some first-rate museums in Moscow and the art galleries are among the finest in the world. Below is a list of the most important ones, together with some of the more specialised collections. If your own special interest is not catered for here, ask your hotel for information. Opening times are the latest available but check before you set out, as there are seasonal and other variations. Unless you are visiting with a tour group, take a detailed guidebook with you – many museums, especially the smaller ones, mark exhibits in Russian only.

The Pushkin Museum of Fine Art (see page 29) houses a celebrated collection of French paintings

Museums and Art Galleries

ALEXANDER PUSHKIN MUSEUM (MUZEY A S PUSHKINA)
Ulitsa Prechistenka 12/2
Dedicated to the life and work of Russia's greatest poet, who died following a duel in 1837. Period house and furnishings, together with paintings, letters and first editions of Pushkin's works. Pleasing, but not as evocative as its St Petersburg equivalent.
Open: Wednesday to Thursday 11.00–19.00hrs, Friday to Sunday 10.00–18.00hrs; Wednesday noon–20.00hrs (summer).
Closed: Monday and Tuesday.
Metro: Kropotkinskaya

◆◆
ANDRONIKOV MONASTERY; ANDREI RUBLYOV MUSEUM OF OLD RUSSIAN ART (SPASO-ANDRONIKOV MONASTYR)
Ploshchad Andronevskaya 10
One of several monastery fortresses guarding the approaches to Moscow, the Andronikov was founded by the Metropolitan Alexey in 1359. The beautifully proportioned white stone building is the Cathedral of the Saviour, dating from 1427. Other buildings worthy of note are the refectory (early 16th century) and the Church of the Archangel Michael and St Alexius (1694–1739). Andrei Rublyov, one of the greatest Russian icon painters, was a monk here. Most of his finest work is now in the Tretyakov Gallery and only traces can be seen in the Cathedral. However, the museum does contain some splendid icons dating from the 15th to 18th centuries, including a work by Dionysius.
Open: daily 10.00–18.00hrs.
Closed: Wednesday and last Friday of each month.
Metro: Ploshchad Ilyicha

◆
BAKHRUSHIN THEATRE MUSEUM (TEATRALNIY MUZEY IM A A BAKHRUSHINA)
Ulitsa Bakhrushina 31/12
More than 200,000 photos, posters, programmes and personal effects illustrating the history of the Russian stage from the 18th century to the present. Items of special interest include Chaliapin's costume for *Boris Godunov* and Nijinsky's dancing shoes. A fascinating collection,

unimaginatively displayed.
Open: Wednesday to Monday noon–18.00hrs.
Closed: Tuesday and last Monday of each month.
Metro: Paveletskaya

◆
BORODINO PANORAMA MUSEUM (MUZEY-PANORAMA 'BORODINSKAYA BITVA')
Kutuzovskiy Prospekt 38
Commemorates the famous battle of August 1812, which was actually fought about 78 miles (125km) to the west of Moscow. The confrontation between the Russian and French forces, which ended in stalemate, is depicted in a 370-foot (115m)-long painting by Franz Roubaud, commissioned to mark its centenary. Close by the museum you can see an exact replica of the hut where Marshal Kutuzov finally decided to abandon Moscow to the French.
Open: Saturday to Thursday 10.30–18.00hrs.
Closed: Friday.
Metro: Kutuzovskaya

◆
CENTRAL MUSEUM OF THE REVOLUTION (MUZEY REVOLYUTSII)
Ulitsa Tverskaya 21
The stone lions guarding the entrance to this museum – formerly the English Club, a favourite haunt of the aristocracy – are mentioned by Pushkin in his poem *Eugene Onyegin*. The exhibition consists of documents, photos, paintings and objects relating to the revolution of 1905 and the February and October revolutions of 1917.

Open: Tuesday to Sunday
10.00–17.30hrs.
Closed: Monday.
Metro: Mayakovskaya

CHEKHOV HOUSE MUSEUM (DOM-MUZEY A P CHEKHOVA)

Sadovaya-Kudrinskaya Ulitsa 6
Chekhov lived here from
1886–90, when he decided to
give up practising medicine to
become a full-time writer. The
study, containing a number of his
personal possessions, is where
he wrote his first play, *Ivanov*,
and many of his short stories.
Open: Wednesday to Friday
14.00–18.00hrs, Tuesday,
Saturday and Sunday
11.00–17.00hrs (summer);
Tuesday to Sunday
11.00–17.00hrs (winter).
Closed: Monday and last day of
each month.
Metro: Barrikadnaya

♦

DON MONASTERY (DONSKOY MONASTYR)

Donskaya Ploshchad 1
Founded by Boris Godunov in
1591 on the site of the last major
confrontation between the
Tatars and Muscovites. The Old
Cathedral has a copy of the Don
Virgin icon, from which the
monastery takes its name. The
New Cathedral and the
defensive walls which surround
it were built by Peter the Great's
sister, Sofiya, in the late 17th
century. The church contains an
impressive iconostasis (screen)
and frescos by Antonio Claudio.
Within the grounds are the
Church of the Archangel
Michael, where members of the
powerful Golitsyn family lie

buried, and the Gate Church of
the Virgin of Tikhvin.
Open: daily 07.00–19.00hrs as it
is a working monastery again.
Metro: Shabolovskaya

♦

GLINKA MUSEUM OF MUSICAL CULTURE (MUZEY IMENI M I GLINKA)

Ulitsa Fadeyeva 4
Named after the founder of
modern Russian music, Milkhail
Glinka, the museum houses
musical instruments, together
with scores, letters and other
items relating to the great
Russian and Western composers
of the 18th and 19th centuries.
Open: Tuesday to Sunday
11.00–18.30hrs.
Closed: Monday.
Metro: Mayakovskaya

KUSKOVO ESTATE MUSEUM (MUZEY-USADBA KUSKOVO)

Ulitsa Yunosti 2
The Sheremetiev family, who
built this estate, once owned
200,000 serfs and more than
three million acres (1,200,000
hectares) of land. The two-
storey wooden palace dates
from 1777 and the interior is
decorated with a dazzling array
of paintings, tapestries and
mirrors. It now functions as a
Ceramics Museum. Other
buildings of note include the
Dutch and Italian houses, the
Hermitage (in French style) and
the Grotto. Sheremetiev's
celebrated company of serf
actors performed in the open-
air theatre near the orangery.
Open: Wednesday to Sunday
10.00–19.00hrs (summer);
10.00–16.00hrs (winter).

Closed: Monday, Tuesday and last Wednesday of each month.
Metro: Ryazanskiy Prospekt

◆

MAXIM GORKY LITERARY MUSEUM (MUZEY-KVARTIRA A M GORKOVO)

Ulitsa Spiridonovka
Devoted to the life and work of Russia's best known socialist writer, the museum formerly belonged to the Director of the Imperial Theatres. On display is an impressive collection of manuscripts, letters, photographs and first editions relating to the author of *The Lower Depths, Mother* and *My Childhood.* The more imposing mansion at

The impressive Don Monastery was once one of Russia's most prosperous, owning 7,000 serfs

number 50 is reputed to be the home of the Rostovs in Tolstoy's novel *War and Peace.*
Open: Wednesday and Friday noon–19.00hrs; Tuesday, Thursday, Saturday and Sunday 10.00–16.30hrs.
Closed: Monday.
Metro: Arbatskaya

◆

MAYAKOVSKY HOUSE-MUSEUM (MUZEY V V MAYAKOVSKOVO)

Proezd Lubyanskiy 3/6
This is where Vladimir Mayakovsky, Futurist poet, playwright and revolutionary, lived from 1919, and where he shot himself 11 years later at the age of 37. The museum contains various artefacts and personal effects, and there are occasional film shows.

CENTRAL MOSKVA

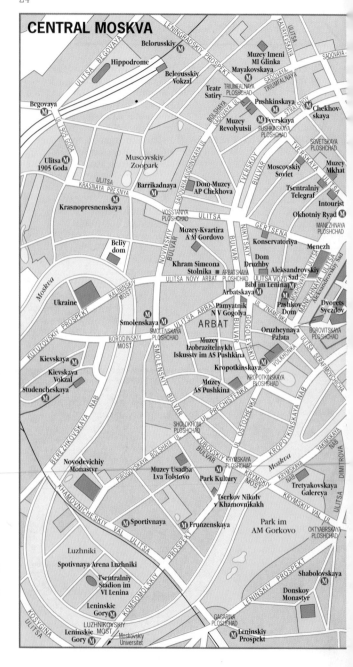

Belorusskiy

ULITSA BEGOVAYA

LENINGRADSKIY PROSPEKT

KALANCHEVSKAYA

ULITSA

SADOVAYA

Hippodrome

Belorusskiy Vokzal

Muzey Imeni MI Glinka

Mayakovskaya

SADOVAYA

TRIUMFALNAYA

Begovaya

ULITSA 1905 GODA

Teatr Satiry

TRIUMFALNAYA PLOSHCHAD

BOLSHAYA SADOVAYA

Pushkinskaya

STRASTNOY

Chekhov-skaya

BOLSHAYA GRUZINSKAYA UL

Muzey Revolyutsii

PUSHKINSKAYA PLOSHCHAD

SOVETSKAYA PLOSHCHAD

Ulitsa 1905 Goda

Muscovskiy Zoopark

ULITSA

TVERSKAYA UL

Moscovskiy Soviet

Muzey Mkhat

ULITSA KRASNAYA PRESNYA

Barrikadnaya

Dom-Muzey AP Chekhova

TVERSKOY

BULVAR

NIKITSKIY

Tsentralniy Telegraf

Intourist

Krasnopresnenskaya

SADOVAYA KUDRINSKAYA UL

VOSSTANYA PLOSHCHAD

ULITSA

GERTSENA

Okhotniy Ryad

MANEZHNAYA PLOSHCHAD

Beliy dom

Muzey-Kvartira A M Gordovo

BULVAR

Konservatoriya

Menezh

NOVINSKIY

Khram Simeona Stolnika

Dom Druzhby

Aleksandrovskiy

Moskva

ULITSA NOVY ARBAT

ARBATSKAYA PLOSHCHAD

ULITSA VOZD

Bibl im Lenina

Sad

MANEZHNAYA ULITSA

Aleksandrovskiy Sad

Ukraine

KALININSKIY MOST

Arbatskaya

Pamyatnik N V Gogolya

UL ZNAMENKA

Pashkov Dom

Dvorets Syezdov

KUTUZOVSKIY PROSPEKT

Smolenskaya

ULITSA ARBAT

ARBAT

GOGOLEVSKIY

Oruzheynaya Palata

UL VOLKHONKA

BOROVITSKAYA PLOSHCHAD

UL SERAFIMOVICHA

Kievskaya

BORODINSKIY MOST

SMOLENSKAYA PLOSHCHAD

SMOLENSKAYA BULVAR

Muzey Izobrazitelnykh Iskusstv im AS Pushkina

Kropotkinskaya

Kievskaya Vokzal

Studencheskaya

Muzey AS Pushkina

KROPOTKINSKAYA PLOSHCHAD

KROPOTKINSKAYA NAB

UL PRECHISTENKA

OSTOZHENKA

YAKIMANSKA NAB

DIMITROVA

BEREZHKOVSKAYA NAB

SHOLOKHOM PLOSHCHAD

Moskva

Novodevichiy Monastyr

PROGOVSKAYA BOLSHAYA UL

ZUBOVSKIY BULVAR

KRYMSKAYA PLOSHCHAD

Muzey Usadba Lva Tolstovo

Park Kultury

KRYMSKIY MOST

KRYMSKAYA NAB

Tretyakovskaya Galereya

KHAMOVNICHESKIY VAL ULITSA

Tserkov Nikolv y Khamovnikakh

KRYMSKIY VAL UL

ULITSA

Sportivnaya

Frunzenskaya

Park im AM Gorkovo

OKTYABRSKAYA PLOSHCHAD

Luzhniki

PROSPEKT

Shabolovskaya

Spotivnaya Arena Luzhniki

Tsentralniy Stadion im VI Lenina

LENINSKIY PROSPEKT

Donskoy Monastyr

KOSIGINA ULITSA

Leninskie Gory

KOMSOMOLSKIY

Leninskie Gory

LUZHNIKOVSKIY MOST

Moskóvskiy Universitet

GAGARINA PLOSHCHAD

Leninskiy Prospekt

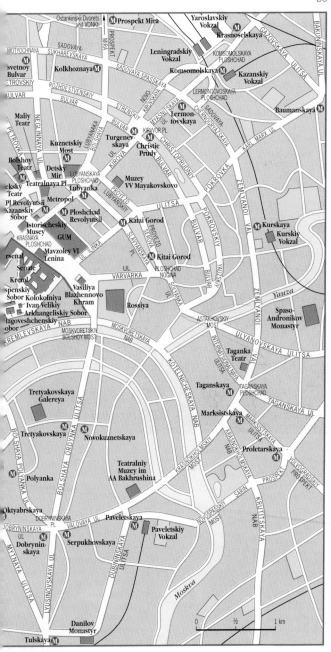

Open: Monday, Tuesday and Friday to Sunday 10.00–17.00hrs; Thursday 13.00–20.00hrs.
Closed: Wednesday.
Metro: Lubyanka

♦♦♦
NOVODEVICHIY CONVENT (NOVODEVICHIY MONASTYR) ✓

Novodevichiy Proezd 1
You will be dazzled by this architectural gem, with its crenellated walls of white brick, red-capped towers and gleaming onion domes.

Founded by Basil III in 1524 to commemorate the capture of Smolensk from the Lithuanians, the convent developed into one of Russia's major religious houses, served by daughters of the nobility. Boris Godunov was proclaimed tsar here in 1598 and, a century later, Peter the Great had his half-sister, Sofiya, imprisoned here for conspiring against him. When Napoleon arrived in 1812 he gave orders for the convent to be blown up but, at the last moment, the nuns extinguished the fuses.

The gleaming white and gold of Novodevichiy Convent, a religious house and occasional prison

The Smolensk Cathedral is the oldest part of the convent and contains some exquisite late 16th-century frescos, a magnificent five-tier iconostasis dating from 1683–6 and a copper font of the same period. Bibles, vestments, silver and other religious treasures are also on view here.

The church of the Dormition, which is open for worship, and the refectory were built in 1685–7. The two Gate Churches, which dominate the northern and southern entrances of the convent, and the 17th-century bell-tower are also worth a look. Just outside the walls is the cemetery, final resting place of Gogol, Chekhov, Eisenstein, Prokofiev, Stanislavsky and the former Soviet leader, Nikita Khrushchev.

Open: May to October: Monday and Wednesday to Sunday 10.00–18.00hrs; November to April: 10.00–17.00hrs.
Closed: Tuesday and last day of each month.
Metro: Sportivnaya

◆◆
OSTANKINO PALACE MUSEUM OF SERF ART (OSTANKINSKIY DVORETS-MUZEY TVORCHESTVA KREPOSTNYKH)

Pervaya Ostankinskaya Ulitsa 5
This estate, like Kuskovo (see page 22) belonged to the fabulously wealthy Sheremetiev family. The wooden palace was designed and constructed entirely by serf labour during the period 1792 and 1798. The interior is a magnificent tribute to these artists and craftsmen. You will marvel at the parquetry, the decorative carvings and the finely wrought crystal chandeliers, and these provide a splendid backdrop to the sumptuous collection of 18th-century furniture, paintings, porcelain and crystal. Sheremetiev's company of 200 actors, all of whom were serfs, performed in the purpose-built theatre which, thanks to an ingenious device which raised the auditorium,

also served as a ballroom. You can also enjoy a stroll in the palace grounds and a visit to the Church of the Trinity, which was commissioned by a previous owner of the estate in 1687. Adjacent to the park are the Botanical Gardens of the Academy of Sciences.
Open: October to April: Monday and Thursday to Sunday 10.00–16.00hrs; May to September: 11.00–17.00hrs.
Closed: Tuesday and Wednesday.
Metro: VVTs

Created by serfs in the 18th century, the Ostankino Palace Museum of Serf art is a show of craftsmanship and splendour; the rich Sheremetievs owned the estate

◆◆◆
PUSHKIN MUSEUM OF FINE ART (MUZEY IZOBRAZITELNYKH ISKUSSTV IM A S PUSHKINA) ✓

Ulitsa Volkhonka 12
This museum is renowned for its collection of French painting, especially of the Impressionist and Post-Impressionist schools. It was founded in 1912, but most of the great works of art now on display were acquired after the Revolution, when the Soviet Government nationalised the private collections of wealthy connoisseurs. If time is short, head for Rooms 17, 18 and 21 on the First Floor, where you will find masterpieces like Manet's *Dejeuner sur l'Herbe* and some of Monet's Rouen Cathedral pictures, as well as paintings by Renoir, Degas, Cézanne, Gauguin, Matisse and some early Picassos. Room 23 (also on the First Floor) displays French and English painting from the early 19th century, including works by Corot, Delacroix and Constable. If you still have time to spare, return to the Ground Floor, where you can choose from among Botticelli and

In 1995 the Pushkin Museum exhibited more than 60 paintings and drawings seized by Soviet troops from occupied Germany after World War II and hidden away in the vaults ever since. The works include pastels by Degas and Manet and a portrait by Corot, long thought to have been destroyed.

Veronese (Room 5); Rubens, Rembrandt and Van Dyck (Rooms 8–10); Murillo and Goya (Room 11); and the French Schools of the 17th and 18th centuries (Room 13). The Pushkin also displays an impressive array of antiquities from Egypt, the Near East, Rome and Byzantium.

In 1996 the Pushkin will display the fabulous classical treasures uncovered in Turkey by German archeologist Heinrich Schliemann in 1873, including what Schliemann took to be King Priam's gold.

Open: Tuesday to Sunday 10.00–19.00hrs.
Closed: Monday.
Metro: Kropotkinskaya

◆
SOVIET ARMED FORCES MUSEUM (MUZEY VOORUZHONNYKH SIL)
Ulitsa Sovietskoy Armii 2
Everything for the military buff. The museum traces the history and development of the Soviet Armed Forces from the Revolution onwards, with special emphasis on the Great Patriotic War (World War II). Among the exhibits are sections of the American U-2 reconnaissance plane brought down over Siberia in 1960, causing President Eisenhower much embarrassment.
Open: 1st and 3rd Tuesday and Wednesday to Sunday 10.00–16.30hrs.
Closed: Monday and 2nd and 4th Tuesday of each month.
Metro: Prospekt Mira

WHAT TO SEE – MOSCOW

◆◆◆ TOLSTOY HOUSE MUSEUM (MUZEY-USADBA LVA TOLSTOVO) ✓

Ulitsa Lva Tolstovo 21
You can feel Tolstoy's presence in every corner of this wonderfully evocative house where the author of *War and Peace* and *Anna Karenina* spent the winters of 1882–1901. The estate museum is also a window onto the world of the late 19th century and life as it was for a member of Russia's privileged classes. Before you go into the main house, explore the outbuildings including the old wing, which contained Tolstoy's publishing office, the barn where he kept the coach and horses and an outdoor kitchen. Sixteen rooms have been preserved as the author left them, including the dining room, where Tolstoy took his evening meal with his wife, Sofiya, and their 13 children, a classroom and nursery, the upstairs hall where high tea was served and where Rachmaninov might play the piano accompanied by Chaliapin and the study where Tolstoy wrote *Resurrection, The Death of Ivan Ilyich* and *The Kreutzer Sonata*. The museum is brought to life as a family home by the wealth of personal effects and ephemera, including Tolstoy's fur coat, bicycle, shoe-making kit and the children's rocking horse.
Open: Tuesday to Sunday 10.00–18.00hrs (summer); Tuesday to Sunday 10.00–16.00hrs (winter).
Closed: Monday and last day of each month.
Metro: Park Kultury

◆◆◆ TRETYAKOV GALLERY (TRETYAKOVSKAYA GALEREYA) ✓

Lavrushinskiy Pereulok 12
The greatest single collection of Russian art in the world, given to the city of Moscow in 1892 by merchant P M Tretyakov. The Gallery, designed by Victor Vasnetsov in a style best described as Russian Art Nouveau, dates from 1900–5. The Tretyakov exhibits almost 50,000 paintings and is most famous for its unrivalled collection of icons, dating to the 11th century. You will find masterpieces by each of the great trio of Russian icon painters: Andrei Rublyov, Dionysius and Theophanes the Greek.
Your next port of call should be the work of the Peredvizhniki or Itinerants, a group of rebel artists of the 1870s, whose founder members included Ivan Kramskoy, Vasily Perov (don't miss his famous portrait of Dostoyevsky) and Fyodor Vasilyev. The Itinerants turned their back on Western fashions in order to concentrate instead on Russian themes. The greatest of them were Ilya Repin, whose best known paintings, include *Religious Procession in Kursk Province, Unexpected Return of a Political Exile* and *Ivan the Terrible and His Son*, and Isaac Levitan, famous for his landscapes. Also in the gallery are paintings by two other artists not to be missed – Mikhail Vrubel and Valentin Serov.
The Tretyakov closed for a complete overhaul in 1985 and

*Named after Tsar Alexander I
Alexander Garden was laid out over
the Neglinnaya River in the early
19th century*

has only recently been re-
opened to the public. The floor
space has expanded and now
includes several older buildings
on Lavrushinskiy Pereulok and a
modern annex in addition to
Vasnetsov's remarkable
building. Art of the Soviet period
as well as contemporary
exhibitions can be found in the
'New Tretyakov' which is on a
different site entirely at Krimskiy
Val Ulitsa 10.
Open: Tuesday to Sunday
10.00–20.00hrs.
Closed: Monday.
Metro: Tretyakovskaya

Other Places of Interest

◆
ALEXANDER GARDEN (ALEXANDROVSKIY SAD)
Manezhnaya Ulitsa
Easily combined with a visit to Red Square. Walk through the gap between the Historical

This intriguing scene is actually the window display of a pet supplies shop in Arbat, an area once home to the tsar's servants

Museum (Istoricheskiy Muzey) and the Kremlin Wall (opposite St Basil's), turn left and you're there. Beneath you is the

Neglinnaya River, which once formed part of the Kremlin moat (a stone bridge still links the Kutafya and Trinity towers). The river was covered over in 1817 and the Gardens were laid out shortly afterwards. By the gate is the Tomb of the Unknown Soldier (Memorial Mogila Neizvestnovo Soldata), guarded by an eternal flame. It is a custom for newly-weds to lay flowers here immediately after their wedding. A little further on is the Obelisk to Revolutionary Thinkers, originally a monument to the Romanov Dynasty, which celebrated its tercentenary in 1913, but was re-designed immediately after the Revolution (the double-headed Imperial eagle was first to go). Continue your stroll through the Gardens and you will eventually come to the Borovitskaya Tower, one of the public entrances to the Kremlin. Across the road is the **Pashkov House and Lenin Library** and the **Manège** is close by.

◆◆◆ ARBAT ✓

The easiest way to reach this delightful part of old Moscow is to walk up Ulitsa Vozdvizhenka and turn left just after the overpass, near the Prague Restaurant. Alternatively, take the Metro and alight at Arbatskaya. This is an area for strolling in, either in the daytime or of an evening. Arbat Street itself, now pedestrianised, was once Moscow's leading shopping street; now it's a favourite haunt of pavement artists, street poets and

musicians. There are bookshops or you can have a bite to eat in one of the many restaurants. The neighbouring streets all have picturesque names: Silver Lane, Biscuit Lane, Carpenters' Lane, Old Stables Lane: a throwback to the days when the Tsar's servants lived here. Later the area was taken over by the aristocracy and some of their imposing residences can still be seen. The Arbat has strong literary associations: Pushkin lived at number 53 for a while, and Gogol's house, 7 Nikitskiy Bulvar, is also close by. There is a famous monument to Gogol (Pamyatnik N V Gogolya) near the Metro station.

◆◆◆ BOLSHOI THEATRE/THEATRE SQUARE (BOLSHOY TEATR/TEATRALNAYA PLOSHCHAD) ✓

Teatralnaya Ploshchad
There has been a theatre on this site since 1780, although the present neo-classical building dates from the mid-19th century. The rather striking bronze quadriga above the portico represents Apollo's chariot being pulled by four horses. The Bolshoi is, of course, the home of the internationally famous opera and ballet company of the same name. In the centre of the square, now reverted to its pre-Revolution name, stands a staue of Karl Marx. To the right of the theatre is the Maly or small theatre (so called to distinguish it from the Bolshoi, which means big) and to the left is the Children's Theatre (Detskiy Teatr).

WHAT TO SEE – MOSCOW

◆◆◆
KREMLIN (KREML) ✓

Kreml
You can visit the Kremlin on your own, or you can join a guided tour. The first alternative is cheaper. (You can buy tickets from the *kassa*, ticket office, in the Kutafya Tower.) You may have to join a lengthy queue to see the State Armoury but, as this is one of the main attractions, equivalent to viewing the Crown Jewels in the Tower of London, you may decide it is worth the wait. The main entrance to the Kremlin is through the Trinity Gate (Troitskaya), where Napoleon entered in triumph in 1812. The tower above the gate was built in 1495 but the tent roof was added almost two centuries later.

The Kremlin (the Russian word *Kreml* means fortress or citadel) is the third such structure on the present site. It occupies nearly 70 acres (28 hectares) on a hill at the confluence of the Moskva and Neglinnaya rivers. The walls stretch for nearly one-and-a-half miles (2.5km) and are up to 65 feet (20m) high and 21 feet (6.5m) thick.

The first Kremlin was built shortly after 1147 by the founder of Moscow, Prince Yuriy Dolgoruky (Long-armed). It was much smaller than the present structure and was built of wood. A second, stone fortress was built in 1367 by Prince Dimitry Donskoi at the time of the Mongol invasions. By the 1470s, the Kremlin had fallen into a state of disrepair and Tsar Ivan III invited leading military architects from Italy to assist in redesigning the fortifications. This explains why the present ring of towers and walls resembles one of the great Renaissance fortresses, like the Castelvecchio in Verona. The later history of the Kremlin is equally eventful. Burnt down in 1547 and sacked by the Tatars in 1571, it was subsequently occupied for a short time by the Poles. Catherine the Great intended to replace it with a new palace complex on neo-classical lines but, fortunately, the project was abandoned. The Kremlin had another narrow escape in 1812 when Napoleon gave orders for it to be blown up. However, it survived, to endure a final siege by the Bolsheviks at the time of the Revolution. On your right as you pass through the Trinity Gate is the glass-fronted **Palace of Congresses (Dvorets Syezdov)**. Opened in 1961, the auditorium, which can accommodate 6,000 people, was the setting for Soviet Party congresses. It is also the second home of the Bolshoi opera and ballet companies, so you may well get an opportunity to have a look around. Squeezed between the Palace and the Kremlin Walls is a narrow street (not open to the public). At the far end you can see the **Poteshniy Palace (Poteshniy Dvorets)**, where Stalin's private apartments were situated and where his wife, Nadezhda Alliluyeva, shot herself in 1932. Now turn around. The long yellow building facing you is the **Arsenal** (also closed to the public). Lined up outside are some of the French cannon captured by the forces of General Kutuzov in the campaign of 1812. Adjoining the Arsenal, at the far end, is the **Nikolskaya Tower**. The Russian heroes Minin and Pozharskiy entered here to expel the Poles in 1612. Just over 300 years later the Bolsheviks stormed the Kremlin here, after a siege lasting several days. The large building nearby with the green dome was once the **Senate** and is now government offices including that of the President. Lenin lived and worked on the third floor.

As with many of the Kremlin towers, the elaborate detail on the Saviour's Tower was a 17th-century addition

WHAT TO SEE – MOSCOW

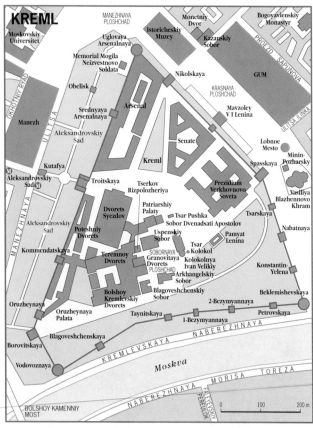

The building nearest to the Saviour's Gate was built by Stalin as the **Presidium** of the Supreme Soviet (Prezidium Verkhovnovo Soveta). To your right is the **Tsar's Cannon (Tsar Pushka)** – the world's largest, over 16 feet (5m) long and weighing in at nearly 36 tons (40 tonnes). Cast in 1586 for the feeble-minded Tsar Fyodor, son of Ivan the Terrible, it has never been fired, but several massive

cannon balls lie ready just in case. Rising behind the cannon is the majestic **Ivan the Great Bell Tower (Kolokolnya Ivan Velikiy)** – for a long time, at 266 feet (81m), the tallest building in Moscow. The gigantic **Tsar's Bell (Tsar Kolokol)**, which stands beside it, is more than 19 feet (6m) high and weighs 189 tons (192 tonnes). It was cast in 1735 but two years later a fire broke out in the Kremlin and a large section broke off when it was doused with water. Return to the Tsar's Cannon and you will see the **Patriarch's Palace (Patriarshiy Palaty)** and the five-domed **Cathedral of the Twelve Apostles (Sobor Dvenadsati Apostolov)**, now the **Museum of 17th-Century Life**. These buildings date from 1645–55 and so are much later than most others in the Kremlin. On the first floor of the Palace/Museum is the Chamber of the Cross, at the time of its construction the largest room in Russia without supporting columns to hold up the roof. The square outside is known as Cathedral Square. Stop here for a while and allow your eyes to feast on the architectural marvels which surround you. The building with the five golden domes is the **Cathedral of the Assumption (Uspenskiy Sobor)** also known as the **Dormition**. Completed in 1479 after only four years, it was designed by Aristotle Fiorovanti of Bologna. Before he embarked on the project he was sent on a tour of Russian churches by Tsar Ivan III and eventually chose the Uspenskiy Cathedral in Vladimir as his model. The result is a near miraculous blend of Russian and Italian styles. This is where the tsars were crowned and the patriarchs and metropolitans of the Orthodox Church laid to rest. While most of the original frescos have been lost or painted over, the overall impression is still quite breathtaking. The walls are covered in artwork of the highest quality, dating mainly from the 17th century, and there

are at least two icons said to be by Dionysius (15th century). The cathedral also contains the throne of Ivan the Terrible, a magnificent piece of wood carving dating from 1551. When the French occupied Moscow in 1812 they turned the cathedral into a stable, plundering its treasures. Huge amounts of silver and gold were hauled away as booty. Much of the silver was later recovered by the Cossacks, who presented the silver and bronze chandelier which now hangs from the dome. The **Church of the Deposition of the Robe (Tserkov Rizpolozheriya)**, built in 1484–6, was at one time the private chapel of the patriarch. The 17th-century frescos and iconostasis are outstanding examples of their kind. The building in front of you as you leave is the **Palace of the Facets (Granovitaya Dvorets)**. Designed by the Italians Marco Ruffo and Pietro Solario in the late 15th century, it takes its name from the rusticated stone façade. The Palace, which is not open to the public, is famous for its magnificent Banqueting Hall, measuring over 598 square yards (500sq m), where the tsars entertained their guests. The **Cathedral of the Annunciation (Blagoveshchenskiy Sobor)** was a private place of worship for the tsar's family and is where royal marriages and christenings took place. It was built by architects from Pskov in 1484–9. Ivan the Terrible later added four more chapels and a number of domes, before giving orders for the entire roof to be covered with gold. Forbidden by Church law to use the main entrance following his fourth marriage in 1572, he built a staircase, porch and chapel of his own, watching the services from behind a screen. The cathedral contains some of the finest artwork in the Kremlin. The frescos, dating from the 16th century, are by Theodosius, son of the famous icon painter, Dionysius. The iconostasis is hailed as the finest in Russia and includes work by Andrei Rublyov and Theophanes the Greek, once thought to have been lost. The five-domed **Cathedral of the Archangel Michael (Arkhangelskiy Sobor)** was built by Alevisio Novi (the Younger) in 1505–8 on the site of an earlier, 14th-century church. All the Tsars and Princes of Muscovy, from 1340 until the beginning of the 18th century, are buried here, with the exception of Boris Godunov whose body lies in Sergievo Posad. The frescos on the walls are mainly 17th-century. Next to the Cathedral of the Annunciation is the **Grand Kremlin Palace (Bolshoy Kremlevskiy Dvorets)**. The present building with its long, yellow and white façade, dates from 1838–49 and was intended

Never fired, the Tsar's Cannon still stands in readiness in the Kremlin

by Tsar Nicholas I to be the Imperial family's Moscow base. The 200-foot (61m)-long St George's Hall, where the guests of the Tsar once danced the night away, is now used for more sober ceremonial. The north wing of the Palace contains the **Terem Palace (Teremnoy Dvorets)**, a superb example of 17th-century architecture. Neither of these buildings is open to the public. As you leave the Grand Kremlin Palace, walk towards the Borovitskaya Tower and you will come to the **Armoury (Oruzheynaya Palata)**. One of the greatest museums of its kind, it is, in effect, a storehouse of Imperial treasures accumulated from the 16th century onwards. Be sure not to miss the Fabergé eggs made for the tsar's family each Easter. Their jewel-encrusted shells open to reveal hidden treasures: a gold replica of the royal yacht, a clockwork miniature of the Siberian Express, a musical box in the shape of the Kremlin. Among the collection of royal paraphernalia are the ivory throne made for Ivan the Terrible and the fur-trimmed Crown of Monomakh, traditionally worn at coronations. Or you may be more interested in the Sevres china, the silverware from the court of Elizabeth I, the Persian armour, the beautifully embroidered vestments and imperial robes, the carriages and sleighs. Don't leave without visiting the Diamond Fund where you can see the crown made for the coronation of Catherine The Great in 1762.

Open: the Armoury, the Kremlin churches and the Museum of 17th-Century Life are open every day except Thursday from 10.00–17.00hrs.

◆◆
LUBYANKA SQUARE (LUBYANSKAYA PLOSHCHAD)
Ploshchad Lubyanskaya
A short walk from the Kremlin, or take the Métro (Lubyanka). The square used to be named after the founder of the Soviet secret police, Felix Dzerzhinsky (actually a Pole). His statue stood in the centre in front of the infamous Lubyanka, former headquarters of the KGB and once the offices of an insurance company. Nearby is the children's store, Detskiy Mir. Tucked away on Malaya Lubyanka Street is the charming Roman Catholic Church of **St Louis**, built in 1830.

◆◆
MANÈGE (MENEZH)
Manezhnaya Ploshchad
Now the Central Exhibition Hall, the Manège was originally a military riding school. It was completed in 1825 to a design by Augustin Betancourt. Wooden girders hold up the roof, which spans 147 feet (45m), without any intermediate supports. Just across Mokhovaya Ulitsa, on either side of Bolshaya Nikitskaya Ulitsa, are the old buildings of Moscow University. The building at the corner of Tverskaya Ulitsa is the National Hotel, one of the most fashionable hotels before the Revolution; Lenin stayed here for several days when the Soviet Government first moved from St Petersburg in 1918.

WHAT TO SEE – MOSCOW

♦♦♦
METRO TOUR ✓

Intourist still offers organised tours of the Metro but this is something you can do quite happily yourself. Avoid the rush hours by visiting the stations after 10.00hrs and before 16.00hrs, or during the evening. The Moscow underground system is one of the great engineering achievements of the Stalin period. The project was entrusted to two of the dictator's leading henchmen, Lazar Kaganovich and the future Soviet leader, Nikita Khrushchev. The first stretch, from Sokolniki to Park Kultury, was opened in 1935. Each station is lavishly decorated with marble, mosaic, stained glass and stainless steel. Chandeliers hang from the ceilings and sculptures and heroic murals adorn the walls. Start your tour at Metro Teatralnaya and try to include Komsomolskaya, Kropotkinskaya, Kievskaya and Mayakovskaya.

♦♦
PASHKOV HOUSE/LENIN LIBRARY (PASHKOV DOM/BIBLIOTEKA IM LENINA)

Mokhovaya Ulitsa
A stone's throw from the Kremlin and the Alexander Garden, the Library, with more than 30 million volumes, is one of the largest in the world. The modern buildings were designed by V A Shchuko and V G Helfreich but of greater interest is the neo-classical Pashkov House, built in 1784–6 for the Governor of Siberia, P Ye Pashkov.

♦♦♦
RED SQUARE (KRASNAYA PLOSHCHAD) ✓

Krasnaya Ploshchad
Surprisingly, the square was given this name long before the Communists came to power; the word *krasnaya* originally meant 'beautiful' as well as 'red'. Begin your tour at Okhotniy Ryad Metro Station. The newly rebuilt Kazan Cathedral (Kazanskiy Sobor) dates originally from 1636 and commemorates the expulsion of the Poles from the Kremlin more than 20 years earlier. It was said that the Russian's owed their victory to the miraculous powers of the Kazan icon of the Mother of God which was carried into battle by their general, Prince Pozharskiy. Bulldozed by Stalin's planners in the 1930s, it is now open once more for worship. The fancifully-decorated dark red building is the Historical Museum (Istorichoskiy Muzey),

The Iberian Gate
Until the 1930s the entrance to Red Square was through the splendid Iberian Gate, a pair of matching white towers, capped by green tent spires. Erected in 1636, the gateway took its name from the tiny chapel dedicated to the Iberian Virgin which stood between its twin arches. Whenever the Tsar came to Moscow it was the custom for him to visit the shrine before entering the Kremlin. The Gate will shortly be re-erected on its original site next to the Historical Museum.

The distinctive, coloured domes make St Basil's Cathedral one of Moscow's best-known landmarks

which was designed in pseudo-Russian style by Vladimir Sherwood in 1878. It has been closed since 1986.

The **Lenin Mausoleum (Mavzoley V I Lenina)** is expected to close to visitors any day. A temporary, wooden mausoleum was erected shortly after Lenin's death in January 1924; the present structure, made from concrete and marble with a mourning band of black labradorite, was completed six years later. At some point the Soviet leader's remains will be buried alongside members of his family in St Petersburg. Behind the Mausoleum and along the Kremlin wall are the graves and memorials of other honoured Communists. Stalin is interred here (his body used to lie next to Lenin's but it was secretly removed in 1961); so is the military leader, Marshal Zhukov, and the first man in space, Yuri Gagarin. Among the

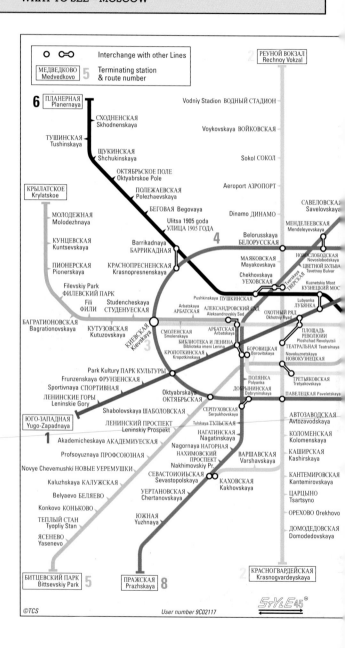

8 АЛТУФЬЕВСКАЯ
Altufyevskaya

Bibirevo БИБИРЕВО

Otradnoe ОТРАДНОЕ

Vladykino ВЛАДЫКИНО

ТРОВСКО-РАЗУМОВСКАЯ
trovsko-Razumovskaya

5 МЕДВЕДКОВО
Medvedkovo

МИРЯЗЕВСКАЯ
niryazevskaya

БОТАНИУЕСКИЙ САД
Botanicheskiy Sad

ДМИТРОВСКАЯ
Dmitrovskaya

ВДНХ VDNKh

АЛЕКСЕЕВСКАЯ
Alekseevskaya

РИЖСКАЯ Rizhskaya

1

ПРОСПЕКТ МИРА
Prospekt Mira

УЛИЦА
ПОДБЕЛЬСКОГО
Ulitsa Podbelskovo

СУХАРЕВСКАЯ
Sukharevskaya

КОМСОМОЛЬСКАЯ
Komsomolskaya

КРАСНЫЕ ВОРОТА Krasniye Vorota

3

УИСТЫЕ
Chistye Prudy

Kurskaya
КУРСКАЯ

ЩЕЛКОВСКАЯ
Shchelkovskaya

ТУРГЕНЕВСКАЯ
Turgenevskaya

УКАЛОВСКАЯ
Chkalovskaya

КИТАЙ-ГОРОД
Kitay-gorod

4

9

Marksistskaya
МАРКСИСТСКАЯ

Ploshchad Ilicha
ПЛОЩАДЬ ИЛЬИЧА

ТАГАНСКАЯ
Taganskaya

СЕРП И МОЛОТ
Serp i Molot

НОВОГИРЕЕВО
Novogireyevo

КРЕСТЬЯНСКАЯ ЗАСТАВА
Krestyanskaya Zastava

7

ВОЛГОГРАДСКИЙ ПРОСПЕКТ
Volgogradskiy Prospekt

ТЕКСТИЛЬЩИКИ Tekstilshchiki

ДУБРОВКА Dubrovka

КУЗЬМИНКИ Kuzminki

РЯЗАНСКИЙ ПРОСПЕКТ
Ryazanskiy Prospekt

ПЕУАТНИКИ Pechatniki

6

ВОЛЖСКАЯ Volzhskaya

ВЫХИНО
Vykhino

ЛЮБЛИНО
Lyublino 9

MOSCOW

UDN.4

select group of foreigners to be honoured here is the American journalist, John Reed (author of *Ten Days that Shook the World*). Behind the Mausoleum is the Senate Tower, built in 1491 by Pietro Solari. To the right is the Nikolskaya or Nicholas Tower, where a drawbridge used to span the Kremlin moat. On the other side of the Mausoleum is the ornate **Spasskaya** or **Saviour's Tower**. Originally designed by Solari in the 15th century, the tent roof was added in 1625. Before the bells were damaged during the Revolution, they played an old Tsarist hymn; now they chime the hours and precede the time signal on Moscow Radio. Religious processions used to pass through this Gate and it was also the entrance used by tsars and foreign ambassadors. No one was allowed in on horseback and even the tsar had to remove his hat.

Opposite the Mausoleum is **GUM (State Universal Store)** once the largest department store in the Soviet Union, and now an attractive shopping mall selling predominantly Western goods. GUM actually dates from 1888–93 and was known originally as the Upper Trading Rows, a reference to some earlier market stalls destroyed during the brief French occupation of 1812.

Between GUM and St Basil's Cathedral is the **Lobnoe Mesto** or **Place of Skulls**. This was where state proclamations were read out and, as the name implies, where criminals were executed. Stenka Razin, who led one of Russia's most famous peasant revolts in 1670, was led to his execution along the street now known as Ulitsa Varvarka. Immediately in front of St Basil's is the **Monument to Minin and Pozharskiy (Minin-Pozharskiy)**. It honours the two leaders from the Time of Troubles who were responsible for expelling the Poles from Moscow and recapturing the Kremlin in 1612.

Originally the Cathedral of the Holy Virgin's Veil by the Moat, **St Basil's (Vasiliya Blazhennovo Khram)** takes its name from Basil the Blessed, the Holy Fool whose remains were interred here shortly after the church was built in 1555–60. Ivan the Terrible ordered its construction to commemorate the historic victory over the Tatars of Kazan in October 1552. The garish colour scheme dates only from the late 17th century; the cathedral was at one time painted white with gilded domes. The interior, with its maze of corridors, chapels and twisting staircases, has to be seen to be believed. It is now a museum.

SPARROW HILLS (VOROBYOVIE GORY)/ LUZHNIKI

Vorobyovie Gory

Known for a long time after the Revolution as Lenin Hills, this spot offers the best panoramic view of central Moscow and is thus ideal for photographs. Close to the river you will see the Central Lenin Stadium (Tsentralniy Stadion im V I Lenina), part of the Luzhniki sports complex where the 1980

Olympics were held. Behind and to the right is the Novodevichiy Convent. The skyscraper on the opposite bank belongs to Lomonsov University. Completed in 1953 in Stalin's favourite Gothic or 'wedding cake' style, it is one of a set which includes the Ukraine Hotel and Foreign Ministry building.

TVER STREET (TVERSKAYA ULITSA)

Tverskaya Ulitsa

The street begins near Okhotniy Ryad Metro Station. Once a narrow twisting lane heading into the countryside, Tverskaya Ulitsa was widened in the 1930s and renamed after the Socialist writer, Maxim Gorky. The skyscraper to your left is the Intourist Hotel. On the next street corner you will see a large, grey building with a revolving globe: this is the Central Telegraph Office (Tsentralniy Telegraf). Opposite, on the street called Kamergerskiy Pereulok, is the **Moscow Arts Theatre (Muzey Mkhat)**, where Chekhov's play *The Cherry Orchard* was first performed. A short walk will bring you to Tverskaya Ploshchad. On the right is the equestrian statue of Prince Yuriy Dolgoruky, the founder of Moscow, and opposite is the building of the Moscow City Council (Moscovskiy Soviet), in Tsarist times the residence of the Governor-General. Continue along Tverskaya Ulitsa, and on your right you will come to the famous food store, once known as Yeliseev's and now, more functionally, as **Gastronom No 1**. Pop in to admire the luxurious late 19th-century décor. A little further on is **Pushkin Square (Pushkinskaya Ploshchad)**. A statue honouring the famous poet stands in the centre. You will also see the gigantic Rossiya Cinema and the offices of *Izvestiya* and the ITAR TASS

press agency. Pass the Metro station and on your left are the railings and gateway of what was formerly the English Club, an exclusive haunt of the nobility. Pushkin mentions the stone lions in his poem *Eugene Onyegin*. This elegant classical building is now The Central Museum of the Revolution (Muzey Revolyutsii).

You could end your walk at Triumfalnaya Ploshchad; the Metro here is named in honour of the poet, Vladimir Mayakovsky and the

Krasnaya Ploshchad means Beautiful or Red Square; the Historical Museum, where tours of the square begin, fits either description

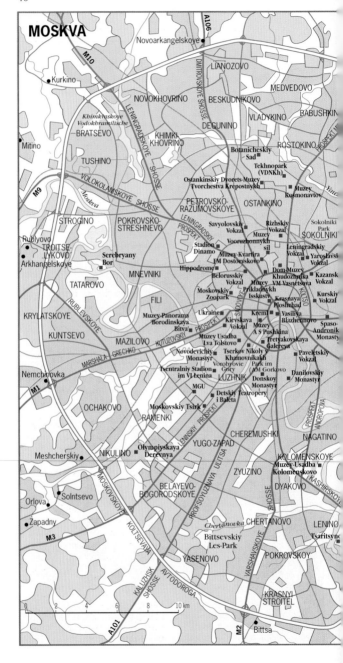

MOSKVA

Novoarkangelskoye

A106

M10

Kurkino

LIANOZOVO

DMITROVSKOYE SHOSSE

MEDVEDOVO

NOVOKHOVRINO

BESKUDNIKOVO

VLADYKINO

BABUSHKIN

LENINGRADSKOYE SHOSSE

Khimkinskoye
Vodokhranilische

DEGUNINO

ROSTOKINO

PROSPEKT

BRATSEVO

KHIMKI-
KHOVRINO

Mitino

Botanicheskiy
Sad

Tekhnopark
(VDNKh)

TUSHINO

VOLOKOLAMSKOYE SHOSSE

Ostankinskiy Dvorets-Muzey
Tvorchestva Krepostnykh

Muzey
Kosmonavtov

M9

Moskva

PETROVSKO-
RAZUMOVSKOYE

OSTANKINO

STROGINO

POKROVSKO-
STRESHNEVO

LENINGRADSKIY PROSPEKT

Savyolovskiy
Vokzal

Rizhskiy
Vokzal

Sokolniki
Park

Rublyovo

TROITSE-
LYKOVO

Arkhangelskoye

Serebryany
Bor

Stadion
Dinamo

Muzey
Vooruzhonnykh
sil

SOKOLNIKI

Leningradskiy
Vokzal

Yaroslavsl
Vokzal

Muzey-Kvartira
F.M Dostoevskovo

MNEVNIKI

Hippodrome

Belorusskiy
Vokzal

Dom-Muzey
Khudozhnika
VM Vasnetsova

Kazansk
Vokzal

TATAROVO

FILI

Moskovskiy
Zoopark

Muzey
Prikladnykh
Isskustv

Krasnaya
Ploshchad

Kurskiy
Vokzal

KRYLATSKOYE

RUBLEVSKOYE

Muzey-Panorama
Borodinskaya
Bitva

Ukraine

KUTUZOVSKIY PROSPEKT

Kiev

Kievskaya
Vokzal

Kreml

Muzey
A S Pushkina

Vasiliya
Blazhennovo

Spaso-
Andronik
Monasty

KUNTSEVO

MAZILOVO

MARSHALA GRECHKO

Muzey Usadba
Lva Tolstovo

Tretyakovskaya
Galereya

Pavel etskiy
Vokzal

Nemchinovka

M1

Novodevichiy
Monastyr

Tserkov Nikoly v
Khamovnikakh

Vorobyovic Park im
Gory
KM Gorkovo

Danilovskiy
Monastyr

Tsentralniy Stadion
im VI Lenina

LUZHNIK

Donskoy
Monastyr

MGU

Detskiy Teatr opery
i Baleta

OCHAKOVO

Moskovskiy Tsirk

PROSPEKT ANDROPOVA

RAMENKI

CHEREMUSHKI

NAGATINO

Meshcherskiy

NIKULINO

Olympiyskaya
Derevnya

LENINSKIY PROSPEKT

YUGO-ZAPAD

PROFSOYUZNAYA ULITSA

KOLOMENSKOYE

Muzey-Usadba
Kolomenskovo

DYAKOVO

KASHIRSKO

Orlova

Solntsevo

ZYUZINO

Zapadny

MOSKOVSKOYE

BELAYEVO-
BOGORODSKOYE

M3

Chertanovka

CHERTANOVO

LENINO

Tsaritsyno

Bittsevskiy
Les-Park

VARSHAVSKOYE SHOSSE

KOLTSEVAYA

YASENOVO

POKROVSKOY

KALUZHSK SHOSSE

AVTODOROGA

0   2   4   6   8   10 km

KRASNYI
STROITEL

A101

M2

Bittsa

WHAT TO SEE – MOSCOW

Tchaikovsky Concert Hall (Kontsertnly Zal im P I Tchaikovskovo) is on the corner, next to the Metro station.

◆◆

VOZDVIZHENKA STREET AND NEW ARBAT STREET (ULITSA VOZDVIZHENKA AND ULITSA NOVIY ARBAT)

Ulitsa Vozdvizhenka; Ulitsa Noviy Arbat

This modernistic thoroughfare was once called Prospekt Kalinina. The ornate building at number 14 was formerly the home of the Moscow millionaire industrialist, Savva Morozov. It is deliberately eclectic in style, combining classical with Renaissance and baroque features. Cross the huge underpass at Nikitskiy Boulevard and you will see the Prague Restaurant on your left, the starting point of the Arbat district. On your right, just past Communications House, is the charming 17th-century church of St Simon Stylites (Khram Simeona Stolpnika), now, alas, looking sadly out of place. The huge tower blocks which now overshadow it house a number of useful shops. In the first block is Dom Knigi (house of books) and Rus-H Supermarket. Further on you will find the Melodiya record store. Across the street are more shops and the Metelitsa nightclub complex, and, much further on, on the corner of Novinskiy Bulvar, the Tropicana restaurant. If you continue to walk as far as the Kalinin Bridge (Kalininskiy Most), you will come to the Ukraine Hotel and Kutuzovskiy Prospekt.

Excursions from Moscow

Tsar Boris Godunov's tomb stands in the shadow of Sergievo Posad's Cathedral of the Assumption and its dazzling blue and gold domes

♦♦♦
SERGIEVO POSAD ✓

This is a marvellous day out, as well as an opportunity to see a little of the Russian countryside, so if you think you have the time to spare, sign up with Intourist right away.

Sergievo Posad is situated 44 miles (72km) northeast of Moscow. As you approach the town by road, the great Trinity Monastery of St Sergius (Troytse-Sergiyeva Lavra) looms into view. Founded in 1340, the fortified walls were added in the 16th century, at the same time as the stunning Cathedral of the Assumption or Dormition, with its blue domes and golden stars. The iconostasis includes a *Last Supper* by the 17th-century master, Simon Ushakov. Next to the cathedral is the tomb of Tsar Boris Godunov and his family.

Sergievo Posad, was for centuries one of the foremost places of pilgrimage in Russia. Prince Dimitry Donskoi came here in 1380 to ask the blessing of the founder, St Sergius, before the battle of Kulikovo. There followed the first Russian victory over the Tatars. The great saint is buried in the Church of the Holy Trinity where you can see icons by two great medieval painters, Danil Chernyi and Andrei Rublyov.

ST PETERSBURG

BACKGROUND

In 1700 the Neva delta and the territory surrounding it still belonged to Sweden. Scattered about the forests and marshland were dozens of tiny settlements and fishing villages, inhabited by Finns and Russians, as well as Swedes. Trade in the region centred on the fortress of Nyenschanz, which overlooked the river bank just opposite the modern Smolniy Convent. (Smolniy itself was occupied by a colony of Russian tar distillers: *smola* means tar, or pitch.) Peter the Great's first attempt to gain a foothold in the region – considered vital for his Westernising ambitions – ended in a humiliating defeat at Narva; but less than three years later his army, now better disciplined and more experienced, besieged and captured Nyenschanz. Only two weeks later, on 16 May 1703, he laid the foundation stone of

Peter the Great, the 'Bronze Horseman', whose ruthless ambition created the city which now bears his name

The tomb of St Petersburg's founder, Tsar Peter I (1672–1725)

what was to be the Peter-Paul Fortress, several miles downstream on an islet known to the local Finns as Yanni-Saari, or Hare Island. The place itself he called *Sanktpeterburg:* St Petersburg. Thousands of serfs from all over Russia, together with Swedish prisoners of war, were drafted to work on Peter's gigantic building site. There was a shortage of wheelbarrows, so the labourers carried the earth in the skirts of their clothes or in bags of rough matting. There was little food, as the area had been devastated by war and the makeshift supply system often broke down. Nor was there much in the way of shelter, as the wooden huts which served as barracks took years to erect in sufficient numbers. As a consequence, untold thousands died of exhaustion and disease in the service of the tsar's boundless ambition. To populate the new capital, Peter issued decree after decree summoning precise numbers of nobles, merchants and artisans and ordering them to build their homes on designated sites, at their own expense and in conformity with his tastes and specifications. They came unwillingly, protesting at the rigours of the climate, the dreariness of the landscape and the measureless gloom of the northern winter. By the time of Peter's death in 1725 there were 40,000 permanent inhabitants.

Early Developments

A number of landmarks were already in place. The stone bastions of the Peter-Paul Fortress had been completed and Trezzini's Cathedral (Petropavlovskiy Sobor) was under construction. The Admiralty was recognisable from its wooden spire, topped by a golden apple and frigate, and there was a Winter Palace. There was a considerable amount of building on Vasilevskiy (Basil's) Island around the Strelka – an Exchange, a Customs House and a number of wharves, as well as the huge ministerial offices or Twelve Colleges, now the University. To the south of the city, at the end of the Great Perspective Road (later Nevskiy Prospekt) was the Church of the Annunciation, the earliest part of the Alexander Nevskiy Monastery to be completed.

As yet this amounted to little more than an urban veneer. The outskirts of the city consisted of dense woodland, and wolves roamed the central area at night. And there were worse natural hazards. St Petersburg was regularly inundated with flood water; the tsar himself nearly drowned on one occasion. There were also devastating fires. It is not surprising, therefore, that when Peter's successor chose to return to Moscow, the nobility was only too delighted to follow suit.

From a City of Wood to a City of Stone

By mid-century, however, St Petersburg was back in favour and it underwent a transformation in the reign of Catherine the Great (1762–96). Vallin de la Mothe's Gostiniy Dvor on Nevskiy Prospekt dates from this period, as does the Tauride Palace (Tavricheskiy Dvorets) and the suburban palaces at Pavlovsk and Tsarskoe Selo. The small Hermitage was built adjoining the Winter Palace, the interior of which Catherine completely refurbished in the classical style. The magnificent Anichkov Palace, overlooking the Fontanka Canal, was presented by

St Petersburg is a city of open spaces: Palace Square, laid out in the 19th century

Catherine to her favourite, Prince Potemkin. The Empress also maintained a lavish court style, which was renowned throughout Europe. The Petersburg 'season' was born.

Catherine's successor, the mad Tsar Paul, built himself a new residence, the Mikhailovskiy Castle, at the eastern end of the Moika and Fontanka Rivers. Terrified of assassination, this martinet of a ruler immured himself in his moated fortress. Only six weeks after he moved in, however, he was smothered in his bed by a band of military conspirators, headed by the Governor of St Petersburg, Count Pahlen.

The 19th Century

Victory over Napoleon in 1812 ushered in a new era of building activity. Some of the most impressive squares in the city were laid out to designs by Carlo Rossi: Palace Square, Arts Square and Senate Square are perhaps the most distinguished. Formerly a parade ground, Senate Square was the setting for an attempted *coup* against Tsar Nicholas I in 1825; the plotters are now regarded as the forerunners of the revolutionary movement. Over the following decades, St Petersburg witnessed an increasing number of demonstrations and terrorist attacks. The first workers' protest took place outside the Kazan Cathedral in 1876 and, five years later, Tsar Alexander II was killed by a bomb while driving along the Catherine Canal (Yekaterinskaya Kanal). The Church of the Resurrection marks the spot. By now St Petersburg was an industrial city with a rapidly expanding workforce. As such it began to attract young Marxist agitators such as V I Ulyanov (Lenin), who, armed with seditious pamphlets and leaflets, made regular forays into the outlying factory suburbs.

City of Revolution

In time this had its effect. When Tsarist troops fired on unarmed demonstrators in Palace Square on 22 January 1905 (Bloody Sunday), the workers responded with strikes and protests which quickly spread to other industrialised regions of Russia. The unrest was renewed in October, culminating in a general strike, which led to the formation of a Soviet (or council) of Workers' Deputies. The Soviet was

Senate Square, scene of rebellion against Tsar Nicholas I in 1825

eventually suppressed, but the tsar was forced to concede Russia's first constitution.

When Germany declared war on Russia in August 1914, the name of the capital was changed to the more Russian-sounding Petrograd. Three years later, a seemingly inexorable political and economic collapse led successively to the revolutions of March and November 1917 and the triumph of Lenin's Bolshevik party. Petrograd provided the setting for most of the dramatic events of that momentous year.

In March 1918 the beleaguered Soviet government abandoned Petrograd and re-established Moscow as the capital. The ensuing civil war reduced the population of the former from 2½ million to 720,000, many fleeing the city to escape starvation. In January 1924, following Lenin's death, Petrograd was renamed Leningrad in his honour.

The Blockade

World War II brought even greater hardship. In September 1941, Hitler's forces surrounded the city, intent on starving it into surrender. The 900 days' blockade which followed resulted in the death of more than 650,000 Leningraders, the majority of whom are buried in the Pickaryovskoye cemetery. To commemorate that terrible period, the Soviets designated Leningrad 'Hero City'.

St Petersburg Today

After the war much of Leningrad and the beautiful palaces which surrounded it lay in ruins. Rebuilding began at once and restoration has been so skilful that the modern visitor can be excused for being ignorant of its post-war desolation. Today the city centre retains its 19th-century appearance, with a complete absence of high-rise devlopments. In contrast, there has been a great deal of expansion in the suburbs, and St Petersburg has more than doubled in size in the last 30 years. Many visitors find St Petersburg more congenial than Moscow. The people appear more relaxed and approachable, while the city seems to have retained something of its Western flavour. Perhaps this is the legacy of Peter the Great.

WHAT TO SEE –
ST PETERSBURG
(S-PETERBURG)

Museums and Galleries

◆
CABIN OF PETER THE GREAT
(DOMIK PETRA)

Petrovskaya Naberezhnaya 6
The log cabin where Peter
supervised the construction of
the city in 1703–9. It took his
soldiers just three days to build.
The museum consists of a study
and dining room with early 18th-
century furnishings. The rigours
of the climate rather than lack of
imagination explain the outer
structure, which now protects
the cabin from the elements.
Easily combined with a visit to
the **Cruiser** *Aurora*.
Open: Wednesday to Monday
11.00–18.00hrs.

Over 70 years ago, the Cruiser
Aurora *fired the signal for the
storming of the Winter Palace.
Now it is a floating museum*

Closed: Tuesday and the last
Monday of the month.
Metro: Gorkoskaya

◆◆◆
CRUISER *AURORA*
(KREYSER *AVRORA*) ✓

*Petrogradskaya Naberezhnaya 4
(opposite the St Petersburg
Hotel)*
Shortly before 22.00hrs on the
night of 7 November 1917 the
Cruiser *Aurora* (then moored
further downstream) fired a
single blank round from its bow
gun in the direction of the
Winter Palace, where the
besieged members of the

Provisional Government were
still holding out. It was the signal
for the insurgents to storm the
Palace, arrest the ministers and
confirm the Bolsheviks in power.
The *Aurora* was built in 1903
and saw active service during
the Russo-Japanese War of
1904–5. At the time of the
Revolution, the *Aurora* was in

*The Hermitage provides an opulent
setting for one of the world's
greatest art collections*

port for a refit, so her place in
history is somewhat accidental.
She was deliberately sunk in
shallow water in 1941, later to
be refloated and converted into
a museum. You can visit the

crew's living quarters and learn more about the ship's fascinating history from an exhibition below deck.
Open: Tuesday to Thursday, Saturday and Sunday 10.30–16.00hrs.
Closed: Monday and Friday.
Metro: Ploschchad Lenina ·

◆
DOSTOYEVSKY MUSEUM (MUZEY-KVARTIRA F M DOSTOEVSKOVO)
Kuznechniy Pereulok 5
This is the apartment where the famous writer wrote *The Brothers Karamazov* and where he lived from 1878 to his death in January 1881. You can see his study and the drawing room where he received visitors during the day (he wrote throughout the night).
Open: Tuesday to Sunday 10.30–17.30hrs.
Closed: Monday and last Wednesday of each month.
Metro: Doestoyevskaya

◆◆◆
HERMITAGE (ERMITAZH) ✓

Dvortsovaya Naberezhnaya 34
One of the greatest, if not *the* greatest art gallery in the world, the Hermitage, or State Hermitage as it is officially known, is also the former residence of the Imperial family. The Winter Palace alone contains well over 1,000 rooms, and its main façade extends more than a mile (1.6km). Add the other buildings in the Hermitage complex and you have 12 miles (19km) of galleries and 3 million exhibits – which is why Intourist offers a

half-day guided tour. This is, however, expensive and you end up somewhat breathless and suffering more than a little from culture fatigue. Better to arm yourself with a plan of the gallery and explore its delights at your own pace. The main entrance to the Hermitage is on the north side of the building, overlooking the river. If you arrive by Metro, walk down Nevskiy Prospekt as far as Admiralty Arch, and Palace Square is on your right. The Hermitage consists of three interlinked buildings: the Winter Palace, the Small Hermitage and the Large Hermitage. The present **Winter Palace (Zimniy Dvorets)** is the fourth on the existing site and was built by Bartolomeo Rastrelli in the baroque style for the Empress Elizabeth in 1754–62. Her successor, Catherine the Great, completely redesigned the interior, bringing it into line with her own tastes. In 1837 the palace was gutted by fire but Nicholas I supervised its immediate reconstruction. The **Small Hermitage** (1764–7) was built for Catherine the Great as a private retreat; at one time the only point of access was through her personal apartments. It became the repository for her collection of Dutch and Flemish masters, the origins of the present gallery. The **Large Hermitage** was built in stages and took almost a century (1770–1860) to complete. A small bridge reminiscent of the Bridge of Sighs in Venice spans the Winter Canal and links the Large Hermitage with Quarenghi's Theatre (closed to

WHAT TO SEE – ST PETERSBURG

the public). The scale of the State Hermitage is stupendous. Besides boasting one of the best art collections in the world, whole floors are devoted to antiquities from Babylon, Assyria, China, Egypt, Greece and Rome, and there are fascinating exhibitions of coins, medals, jewellery and porcelain. But you are best advised to start with the European art, for which the gallery is most famous. The Hermitage's outstanding collection of French painting of the 19th and 20th centuries is on the second floor of the Winter Palace's south wing. Apart from works by Monet, Cézanne, Degas, Renior and Gauguin, the Hermitage possesses 35 canvases by Matisse (Rooms 343–5) and some early masterpieces by Picasso (Rooms 346–7). To embark on a tour of the first floor of the Winter Palace is to journey into the pre-revolutionary past. The Fore Hall, near the top of the Jordan staircase, is where the tsar's most favoured guests used to gather before dining in the sumptuous splendour of St George's Hall, which links the Palace and the Small Hermitage (Room 198). Once sated, they would drift back to the Nicholas Hall (Room 191) for the formal Imperial ball. Next-door-but-one is the Malachite Hall, where, on the night of 7/8 November 1917, Alexander Kerensky presided over his last cabinet meeting. (His colleagues were arrested in the White Dining Room and frog-marched to the Peter-Paul Fortress.) The adjoining suite of rooms was occupied by the ill-fated Nicholas II and his family,

though they preferred to avoid St Petersburg after the first rumblings of revolution in 1905. Particularly impressive is the Gothic Library (Room 178). The rooms at the far end of this wing were used by Alexander II. In 1880 a revolutionary, posing as a workman, infiltrated the Palace and managed to plant a bomb underneath the tsar's dining room (Room 161). Eleven people were killed in the explosion but Alexander himself escaped. Only a year later, however, his sleigh was blown up as he was driving home and his mortally injured body was brought back to this part of the Palace, where he died. Return now to the Jordan staircase, so called because this was the route the tsar took each 6 January for the ceremonial blessing of the River Neva. The splendid Gallery of 1812 has portraits of all the victorious generals and senior officers. This section of the Palace is known as the Great Enfilade. The Hall of St George (Room 198) was referred to earlier. This vast chamber was once the Imperial throne room and here Nicholas II inaugurated Russia's pre-revolutionary parliament, the State Duma, in 1906. The first floor of the Large Hermitage is devoted to art of the Italian, Flemish and Spanish schools, and includes two Leonardos (Room 214), several Titians (Room 221), a Michelangelo (Room 230) and 26 Rembrandts, as well as works by Velasquez, El Greco, Rubens, Canaletto and Tiepolo.
Open: Tuesday to Sunday 10.30–18.00hrs. *Closed*: Monday.

◆
HISTORY OF LENINGRAD MUSEUM (RUMYANTSEVSKIY DVORETS)

Naberezhnaya Krasnogo Flota 44
This museum, in the former Rumyantsev Palace, concentrates on the post-revolutionary history of the city and includes a special exhibition on the 900 days in 1941–4 when Leningrad was besieged by the Germans.
Open: Monday, Tuesdays, and Thursday to Sunday 11.00–16.00hrs.
Closed: Wednesday.

◆
MARBLE PALACE (MRAMORNIY DVORETS)

Millionaya Ulitsa
This former palace was built by Catherine the Great in the late

Built in the 18th century, the present Winter Palace is the fourth to stand on its site

18th century for her favourite, Count Grigory Orlov and was later occupied by one of the Romanov Grand Dukes. The architect was Antonio Rinaldi. What remains of the sumptuous interior (the Marble Hall and Grand Staircase) is now the backdrop for temporary art exhibitions organised by the Russian Museum.
Open: Monday and Wednesday to Sunday 10.00–18.00hrs.
Closed: Tuesday.

◆◆◆
PETER-PAUL FORTRESS (PETROPAVLOVSKAYA KREPOST) ✓

Petropavlovskaya Krepost 3
Situated on Zayachy or Hare Island, the fortress was built in 1703–10 to give protection against the Swedes. It was, in fact, never needed for that purpose. Instead, it became one

CENTRAL S- PETERBURG

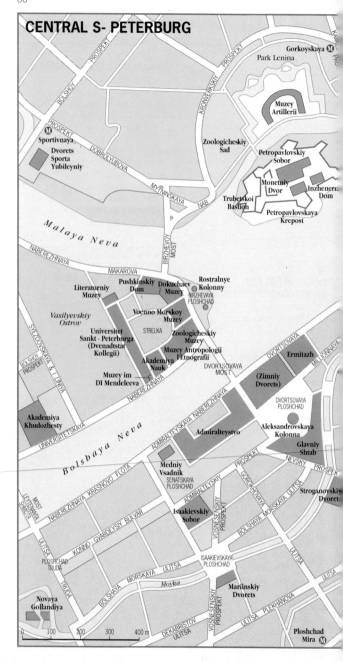

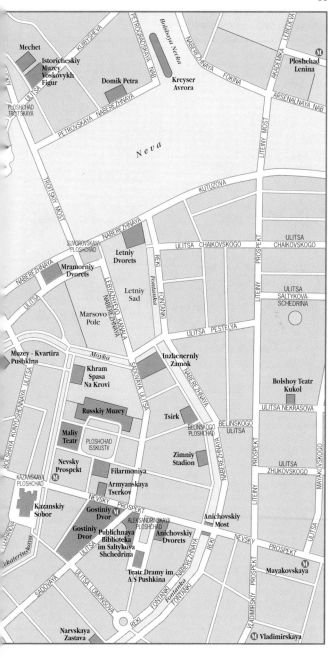

WHAT TO SEE – ST PETERSBURG

The Peter-Paul Fortress has a grim and notorious past

of the most notorious prisons in the Russian Empire. The Engineer's House (Inzhenerniy Dom), beyond the Petrovskiy Gate, is now an architecture museum, with maps and plans showing how the city was built. At the centre of the Fortress complex is the 18th-century Cathedral of SS Peter and Paul (Petropavlovskiy Sobor). Replacing a wooden church, the present building was designed by Domenico Trezzini in 1713 and completed 20 years later. The golden spire, which gleams magically in the sunlight, is a landmark and used to be the tallest structure in the city. Inside the church are the tombs of most of the tsars and tsarinas

from the 18th century onwards, including Peter the Great himself. Opposite the Cathedral is the Mint (Monetniy Dvor), which still issues commemorative coins and medals. The Trubetskoi Bastion is now a museum. In former times however, it was one of Russia's grimmest prisons – generations of revolutionaries wasted away in its cells and dungeons, though one of its earliest victims was Peter the Great's own son, beaten to death here in 1718, possibly with his father's active participation! Dostoyevsky was incarcerated here for a time; so was the demented Sergei Nechaev, who succeeded, nevertheless, in converting several of his gaolers to the revolutionary cause. (Nechaev was the inspiration for

Dostoyevsky's novel *The Possessed*.) Among other notable occupants of the Trubetskoi Bastion were Leon Trotsky, imprisoned in the wake of the 1905 revolution, and Lenin's elder brother, Alexander, subsequently hanged for his role in a conspiracy to murder the Tsar. Behind the Fortress, on the mainland, is the Artillery Museum (Muzey Artillerii), with Lenin Park (Park Lenina) on one side and the Zoo (Zoologicheskiy Sad) on the other.
Open: Thursday to Tuesday 11.00–17.00hrs.
Closed: Wednesday.
Metro: Gorkovskaya

◆◆◆
PUSHKIN MUSEUM (MUZEY-KVARTIRA PUSHKINA) ✓

Naberezhnaya Reki Moiki 12
Wonderfully evocative and something of a shrine for Russians, this is where the poet lived from the autumn of 1836 and where he was brought home to die following a duel with Baron d'Anthes in January 1837. The rooms have period furnishings and many of Pushkin's personal possessions are on display.
Open: Monday and Wednesday to Sunday 10.30–18.00hrs.
Closed: Tuesday.

◆◆◆
RUSSIAN MUSEUM (RUSSKIY MUZEY) ✓

Inzhenernaya Ulitsa 4
Unlike the Hermitage, the Russian Museum specialises in Russian art, mainly from the 18th century onwards. There are well over 100 rooms, so it's essential to home in on the important items: the priceless collection of icons including work by the greatest exponent of the art form, Andrei Rublyev (1340–1430); paintings by Levitsky, the 'Russian Gainsborough'; works by the 19th-century artist, Ilya Repin, including the famous *Volga Boatmen*. There are some fine landscapes by Korovin and a friend of Chekhov's, Isaac Levitan. Don't miss the wonderful portraits of Diaghilev and Chaliapin by Leon Bakst, or the great modern art of Larionov, Goncharova, Kandinskiy and Malevich in the adjoining Benois Wing (expect changing exhibitions).
The museum is housed in what used to be the Mikhailovskiy Palace, built in 1819–25 for the Grand Duke Mikhail Pavlovich, brother of Tsars Alexander I and Nicholas I. It was converted to its present function by Nicholas II at the end of the 19th century.
Open: Wednesday to Monday 10.00–18.00hrs.
Closed: Tuesday.
Metro: Nevskiy Prospekt

◆◆
RUSSIAN POLITICAL HISTORY MUSEUM (MUZEY VOSKOVYKH FIGUR)

Ulitsa Kuibysheva 4
This imposing mansion once belonged to the great ballerina, Mathilde Kseshinskaya, a former mistress of Nicholas II. When she fled during the March Revolution, the building was taken over by the Bolsheviks, who made it their Party headquarters. There are two

exhibitions: a waxworks display containing a dozen historical figures including every Russian leader from Nicholas II to Boris Yeltsin; and an exhibition entitled 'Russia, terror or democracy?' which reappraises the activities of the political opposition movement to the Tsarist regime. The artefacts include a policeman's uniform, assorted bomb-making equipment, terrorist death threats and handcuffs. (Handy for **Cabin of Peter the Great**, **Cruiser *Aurora*** and **Peter-Paul Fortress**.)

Open: Friday to Wednesday 10.00–17.30hrs.
Closed: Thursday.
Metro: Gorkovskaya

Other Places of Interest

> ◆◆◆
> ### ALEXANDER NEVSKIY MONASTERY (ALEKSANDRO-NEVSKIY LAVRA) ✓

Situated at the far end of Nevskiy Prospekt, this working monastery, founded by Peter the Great in 1713, is one of the most important in Russia. The Cathedral of the Trinity is open to the public (sung services are held Sundays at 10.00hrs). Also within the monastery complex is the **Museum of Town Sculpture**, (open every day except Thursday). Many of the nations' writers and musicians are buried in the cemetery here, including Dostoyevsky, Tchaikovsky and Rimsky-Korsakov.

Open: daily 08.00hrs–14.00hrs.
Metro: Ploshchad Aleksandra Nevskogo

◆◆
ARTS SQUARE (PLOSHCHAD ISSKUSTV)
Ploshchad Isskustv
Off the Nevskiy Prospekt near Gostiniy Dvor. Both the Russian Museum and Maly Theatre (Maliy Teatr) are located here and the Philharmonic Hall is just around the corner in Mikhaylovskiy Street. The square was laid out by Carlo Rossi in the 1830s and was intended to set off the Mikhailovskiy Palace (now the museum). In the centre is a statue of Pushkin. The concert hall, formerly the Club of the Gentry, was taken over by the Russian Musical Society in 1859.

◆
MARS FIELD (MARSOVO POLE)
Marsovo Pole
This huge square by the Trinity Bridge was once a military parade ground. It now commemorates those killed in the Revolution and Civil War. Occupying one side of the square are the former barracks of the Pavlovskiy Regiment, whose troops were the first to mutiny during the March Revolution of 1917.

> ◆◆◆
> ### NEVSKIY PROSPEKT ✓

St Petersburg's majestic main street was laid out in the 1750s and was formerly known as the Great Perspective Road. It stretches fully three miles (5km), from the Admiralty to the Alexander Nevskiy Monastery, and is easily reached either by Metro or tram. All the major

Named after a warrior and saint who defeated the Swedes in 1240: the Alexander Nevskiy Monastery

stores are located here, as is a wide variety of cafés, theatres and cinemas. Starting from the Admiralty end, the first street to the right is Malaya Morskaya Ulitsa (formerly Gogol Street), commemorating the author of *Dead Souls* and *The Inspector General*, who lived at number 17. Number 13 was the last residence of the composer, Tchaikovsky, who died of cholera after drinking unboiled tap water (so be warned!). The next street is Bolshaya Morskaya Ulitsa, where you will find the Astoria Hotel. Fabergé's shop was also situated here, at number 24. Continuing along Nevskiy Prospekt, the building

WHAT TO SEE – ST PETERSBURG

on the right hand side with the large neon sign is the Barrikada Cinema, formerly the Club of the Nobility. Opposite, by the Moika Bridge, is the **Literature Café**, formerly the highly fashionable **Wulf et Beranger**. This is where Pushkin met his duelling second before heading off for his fatal encounter with Baron D'Anthes. **Pushkin's house**, now a museum, is nearby at 12 Moika Embankment. Cross the bridge and on your left is the Dutch church, one of a number of foreign churches on Nevskiy Prospekt. The green and white building on the

Pushkin strikes a declamatory pose outside the Russian Museum

opposite corner is the **Stroganov Palace (Stroganovskiy Dvorets)**, reputed to be one of the finest in St Petersburg. Before the Revolution the Stroganovs owned one of the best private art collections in Russia. This has now been swallowed up by the Hermitage. St Peter's Lutheran Church is at number 22–4. Opposite is one of St Petersburg's most distinguished buildings, the **Kazan Cathedral (Kazanskiy Sobor)**. Completed in 1811 to a design of Voronikhin, the imposing colonnade is modelled on St Peter's in Rome. Kazan Square was a favourite meeting point for revolutionaries. Across the street, occupying the former

premises of the Singer Sewing Machine Company, is Dom Knigi, the city's major book store – note the distinctive globe on the roof. On your left as you cross the Kazan Bridge is the Catherine Canal. The large ugly building at the far end is the **Church of the Resurrection (Khram Spasa 'Na Krovi')**, built on the spot where Tsar Alexander II was assassinated in 1881. A little further up on the right hand side is the long façade of **Gostiniy Dvor**, or **Merchant's Yard**. Completed in the reign of Catherine the Great, when renovated it will resume its role as St Petersburg's premier shopping mall, the equivalent of GUM in Moscow, and just as crowded. The street running off to your left is Mikhaylovskiy Street, where both the Philharmonic Hall and the Grand Hotel Europe are situated. **Arts Square** is at the far end. Continue along Nevskiy Prospekt and on your left you will see the blue and white Armenian church, followed by the Passazh Department Store. A little higher up, at number 52, is **Yeliseev's** food store, which still retains something of its pre-revolutionary opulence. The next major intersection, just beyond Gostiniy Dvor, is Sadovaya Street. Cross it and the building on your right is the **Saltykov-Shchedrin Public Library (Publichnaya Biblioteka im Saltykova Shchedrina)**, a favourite haunt of, among others, Tolstoy and Lenin. Alexandra Square, designed by Carlo Rossi in the 1820s, is named after the elegant yellow building where

Gogol's *Government Inspector* was first performed. In the garden outside is a statue of Catherine the Great. On the far side of the square is the **Anichkov Palace (Anichovskiy Dvorets)**, which once belonged to Catherine the Great's favourite, Prince Potemkin. The **Anichkov Bridge (Anichovskiy Most)**, which spans the Fontanka River, is famous for the four rearing horses which decorate each corner. The Fontanka is probably the most suitable point to conclude your tour of Nevskiy Prospekt. If you wish to carry on, you will eventually come to Ploshchad Znamenskaya, where the Moscow Railway Station is situated. From here you can take the Metro back into town or, alternatively, proceed to the Alexander Nevskiy Monastery, but this is a good walk.

◆◆◆
PALACE SQUARE/THE ADMIRALTY (DVORTSOVAYA PLOSHCHAD/ ADMIRALTEYSTVO)
Dvortsovaya Ploshchad
This splendid square, with the green and white **Winter Palace** as its focal point, was laid out in its present form by Rossi in the 1820s. On the far side, opposite the Palace, is the former Main Staff building of the Russian Army, actually two buildings linked by a gigantic arch. At the centre of the square is the **Alexander Column (Aleksandrovskaya Kolonna)**, made from red granite and erected to commemorate Russia's defeat of Napoleon in 1812. Military parades were held here and the tsar would

cross the square on horseback to review his troops. In January 1905 Palace Square was the scene of a massacre, when soldiers opened fire on unarmed demonstrators gathering to present a petition to the tsar. The incident, known in Russian history as Bloody Sunday, sparked off the revolution of that year. Twelve years later, Bolshevik forces began their attack on the Winter Palace from this point, though there was no frontal assault of the kind portrayed by Eisenstein in the film *October*.

The fine classical building immediately to the west of the square is the **Admiralty**. Designed by Zakharov at the beginning of the 19th century, it is instantly recognisable by its gilded spire, crowned by a weather-vane in the shape of a sailing ship. The Admiralty stands on the site of Peter the Great's first shipyard, constructed in 1704.

◆◆◆
ST ISAAC'S CATHEDRAL AND SQUARE (ISAAKIEVSKIY SOBOR/ISAAKIEVSKAYA PLOSHCHAD) ✓

Isaakievskaya Ploshchad
There has been a church on this site since 1710 but the present building dates from the early 19th century. It was finally opened in 1858. The vast interior can accommodate 14,000 worshippers, and is lavishly, if rather tastelessly, decorated. Note the iconostasis, with its malachite and lazurite columns. The cathedral has an exhibition which traces its history but in Russian only.

Don't leave without climbing the dome which offers a magnificent panoramic view of the city. Tickets are on sale inside the building but photography, unfortunately, is not permitted.
Open: Thursday to Tuesday 11.00–19.00hrs.
Closed: Wednesday.
The most important building in St Isaac's Square lies on the south side, across the Siniy Most, or Blue Bridge. This is the **Mariinskiy Palace (Mariinskiy Dvorets)**, where the Tsar's Council of Ministers used to meet before the Revolution. In 1917 it was taken over by the Provisional Government. Nowadays it serves as St Petersburg's Town Hall.

◆◆
SENATE SQUARE (SENATSKAYA PLOSHCHAD)

Senatskaya Ploshchad (near St Isaac's Cathedral)
In Soviet times this was called Decembrist Square to commemorate the liberal guards officers who, in December 1825, tried unsuccessfully to stage a *coup d'état* against Tsar Nicholas I. The rebellion was easily put down as workmen watched in amazement from the scaffolding of St Isaac's Cathedral. Five of the conspirators were hanged and many more exiled to Siberia. Formerly a parade ground, Senate Square was laid out by Carlo Rossi in the 1830s. Falconet's statue of Peter the Great, known as the 'Bronze Horseman', occupies a central position. The inscription on the base reads 'To Peter the First

from Catherine the Second. MDCCLXXXII. The statue was made famous by Pushkin in a poem of the same name.

◆
SMOLNIY INSTITUTE (SMOLNIY INSTITUT)

Situated next door to the colourful Smolniy Convent, the Smolniy Institute was originally a

Crowds follow the broad sweep of St Petersburg's Nevskiy Prospekt

school for daughters of the nobility. In 1917 it became the premises of the Petrograd Soviet and of the Bolshevik Central Committee. It was to Smolniy that Lenin came in disguise to oversee the Communist seizure of power. His government continued to meet here until March 1918, when it moved to Moscow. In December 1934 the Leningrad party boss, Sergei Kirov, was assassinated here – the event

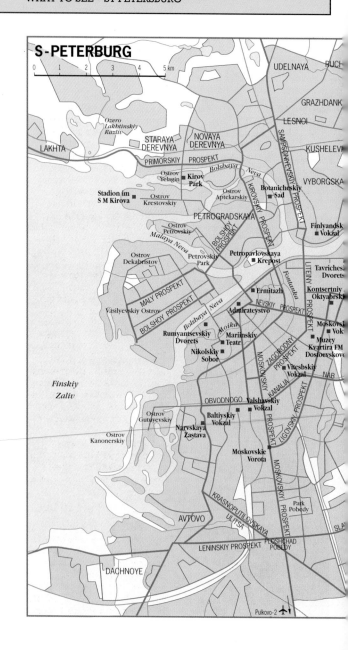

which preluded Stalin's purges. The Smolniy Institute is now the Mayor's office.

◆
VASILEVSKIY ISLAND (VASILEVSKIY OSTROV)

A short walk across Palace Bridge, Vasilyevskiy or Basil's Island was to have been the centre of Peter the Great's new city. Instead it became a residential district and was known in the 19th century as the German quarter. From the Strelka (arrow head) there is a magnificent view of the city. The **Rostral Columns (Rostralnye Kolonny)**, which rise from the square, mark the site of the original port and once served as lighthouses. The white-columned building, once the Stock Exchange, is now the Central Naval Museum. Next door is the Zoological Museum. Further round, on the Malaya Neva Embankment, is the **Literary Museum (Literaturniy Muzey)**, formerly the Customs House. On the other side of the Strelka, beyond the Zoology Museum, are the **Museum of Ethnography and Anthropology (Muzey Antropologii l'Etnografii)** and the **Academy of Sciences (Akademiya Nauk)**, founded by Peter the Great in 1725.

River Tours

Though the rivers and canals of St Petersburg are iced over for much of the winter, boat travel is a highly enjoyable way to see the city in summer. The cheapest ride takes you from **Naberezhnaya Krasnovo Flota** (Red Fleet Embankment, near

the statue of the Bronze Horseman) to the **Smolniy Institute**. This will give you an excellent view of the Strelka, the Hermitage, the Peter-Paul Fortress, the Summer Gardens and the area around Smolniy. Alternatively, you can pick up a boat at the **Anichkov Bridge** and tour the inland waterways and canals. In summer months, there are night boat tours on the Neva and canals (departing from the Dvortsovaya Embankment at 22.00hrs or the Anichkov Bridge, departing midnight).

The magnificent blue and white Cathedral of the Smolniy Convent

Excursions Outside St Petersburg

Many firms specialise in tours of the tsars' summer residences and are well worth subscribing to during your stay.

The two most interesting palaces are **Tsarskoe Selo** (Tsar's village) and **Peterhof** (Peter's Palace). All the palaces were looted before being blown up by the Germans during the war, but each one has now been painstakingly restored.

◆◆
PAVLOVSK
Pavlovsk is only a few miles from Tsarskoe Selo and often included in the same excursion. If you are travelling independently, take the number 370 bus from Tsarskoe Selo; or the train from Vitebsk station in St Petersburg, then bus number 383 or 473. This palace, a little matter of 1,300 acres (526 hectares), was a gift from Catherine the Great to her son Paul. It was designed along classical lines by Scotsman Charles Cameron and completed in 1786. The Halls of Peace and War on the first floor are among the most attractive in the palace. The grounds are magnificent.
Open: Saturday to Thursday 10.00–17.30hrs.
Closed: Friday.

◆◆◆
PETERHOF (FORMERLY PETRODVORETS) ✓

Peterhof is on the southern shore of the Gulf of Finland, 18 miles (29km) from St Petersburg. The fastest route in the summer is along the Malaya Neva, by hydrofoil (May to September departing from the Hermitage pier). Otherwise take the train from the Baltic station in St Petersburg (Naberezhnaya Obvodnovo Kanala; Metro: Baltiskaya), then buses 350, 351, 352 or 356 from Noviy Petergof Station.

Peterhof was first occupied by Peter the Great while he was overseeing work on the great fortress of Kronstadt, nearby. A visit to Versailles in 1717 transformed his relatively modest ambitions. The small palace of **Monplaisir**, which overlooks the sea, was completed by the time of Peter's death in 1725. The Great Palace, on the other hand, was virtually rebuilt by Rastrelli and only completed in 1754. The *pièce de resistance* is the Great Cascade, a glorious display of fountains, terraces and waterfalls descending to the sea (currently being restored).
Open: Tuesday to Sunday 10.30–18.00hrs.
Closed: Monday and the last day of each month.
Monplaiser closed Wednesday and November to April.

◆◆◆
TSARSKOE SELO ✓

If you want to make your own way to Tsarskoe Selo, take the train from St Petersburg's Vitebsk Station (Zagorodny Prospekt; Metro – Pushkinskaya) to Dyetskoye Selo, then buses 371 or 382, which go directly to the palaces. Alternatively, Intourist will take you there by coach and will supply an English-speaking tour guide.

WHAT TO SEE – ST PETERSBURG

Tsarskoe Selo is situated about 15 miles (25km) south of St Petersburg. During the Soviet era it was named after the great Russian poet, Pushkin, who went to school here (the Lyceum) and owned a *dacha* (summer home) in the vicinity. In Tsarist times, Tsarskoe Selo was a fashionable haunt of the aristocracy, who were anxious to be near the imperial family and to escape the noxious air and oppressive climate of the capital. After the Revolution of 1905, Nicholas II and his family lived here more or less permanently and spent several months under house arrest following the March Revolution of 1917. Pushkin, as it was then known, was overrun by the Germans in 1941; when they left three years later the palaces were devastated.

The Catherine Palace was built in baroque style by the great Italian architect, Bartolomeo

Waterfalls, terraces and gardens form a majestic symmetry in the Great Palace of Peterhof

Rastrelli, in the 1750s (he later went on to design the Winter Palace). It replaced an earlier building, commissioned by the Empress Elizabeth and named after her mother, the wife of Peter the Great. Elizabeth's successor, Catherine the Great, subsequently called in another architect, the Scotsman, Charles Cameron, to redesign the interior in the classical style to which she was partial. The decoration is magnificent throughout. The walls of the Picture Hall, designed by Rastrelli, are covered with more than 130 paintings, most of them originals. Exquisite stucco bas-reliefs adorn the Green Dining Room, and silks with Chinese motifs give the Chinese Blue Drawing Room its name. Adjacent to the palace are the baths, sumptuously decorated in agate and jasper. The Ulitsa Vasenko leads from the side of the palace, past the Pushkin statue to the yellow and white Alexander palace, residence of Nicholas II from 1905 to 1917. The Catherine Park, which is a delight to stroll in during summer, reveals the essential frivolousness of the age. There is a Turkish bath made to resemble a mosque, a Chinese pavilion and a cemetery where Catherine buried her favourite pet dogs.

Open: daily 10.00–17.00hrs.
Pushkin's Dacha:
Open: Wednesday to Sunday 11.00–17.00hrs.
Closed: Monday and Tuesday.
Pushkin Lyceum:
Open: Wednesday to Monday 10.30–16.30hrs.
Closed: Tuesday.

PEACE AND QUIET

Countryside and Wildlife in Moscow and St Petersburg by Paul Sterry

Russia's geography ranges from snow-capped mountain peaks to deserts and from inland seas to the tundra of the Arctic coast. Although visitors to Moscow and St Petersburg can only hope to experience a fraction of this variety, many interesting habitats lie within a short distance of these cities. Visitors with an interest in natural history may feel a little frustrated. At the time of writing, trips to nature reserves cannot be made without prior arrangement with the authorities. If you wish to visit a specific site, contact Intourist well before you leave home, but be prepared for disappointment. Alternatively, you could join one of the few

The grey and black hooded crow

specific natural history tours organised by companies based in the west.

Without prior arrangements, the best opportunities for observing wildlife are had by joining excursions to the countryside, rural villages or stately parks; as long as you are out of the urban areas there will be something to see. By referring to the habitats covered later in the text and recognising the type in which you find yourself, you can get a good idea of what to look for.

In and Around Moscow

Most visitors to Moscow come to marvel at the splendour of its architecture and to experience a different culture, but the city's parks make a pleasant and relaxing contrast to the buildings. Although they lack the species diversity of woodlands in the surrounding countryside, sites such as Gorky Park or Izamilovo Park sometimes harbour a surprising variety of birds.

PEACE AND QUIET

The Botanic Gardens of the Academy of Sciences at Ostankino have patches of semi-natural mixed woodland, along with a wide variety of plant species from elsewhere in Russia. Hooded crows and starlings are resident, but during migration time in spring and autumn, birds such as barred warblers, willow warblers, greenish warblers and red-breasted flycatchers may turn up.

Because Moscow lies well inland, the climate is distinctly continental, with hot summers and cold winters. The severity of the winter, which drives many species of birds south to warmer climates, freezes the Moskva River. However, in summer, a boat trip is a good way to see the sights. Parties of swifts scream overhead and the river sometimes hosts black-headed gulls and small groups of marsh terns.

St Petersburg

St Petersburg's position on the coast ensures that it generally has a milder climate than Moscow, although this still does not prevent the Neva River from freezing during the winter months. Parks and gardens are plentiful, and many serve as a haven for a variety of birds as well as weary tourists. Close to the city centre, the Summer Gardens, Lenin Park, which contains the Zoological Gardens, Kirov Park and Moskovskiy Park Pobedy harbours trees and shrubs attractive to wildlife. Primorsky Park Pobedy on Krestovsky Island and further afield the

gardens in Tsarskoe Selo also merit a visit. Butterflies are attracted to ornamental flowers, and resident hooded crows are sometimes joined by summer visitors such as robins, thrushes and pied, spotted or red-breasted flycatchers.

Excursions to the Island of Kizhi on Lake Onega should give you the opportunity to see waterbirds such as grebes and ducks; and a trip to the Kirov Islands or a cruise in the Gulf of Finland may offer views of seals or seabirds such as great black-backed gulls, Caspian terns, black guillemots, eiders, cormorants or divers.

The Russian Steppe

To the south of Moscow there once lay a great bank of temperate grassland known as the steppes, which stretched from the Polish border to China. Although much of the natural vegetation has disappeared under the plough, there are pockets of steppe vegetation that still persist in nature reserves, and many of the less intensively farmed regions retain some of their former wildlife features.

Sheep's fescue, feather grass and wormwood are the dominant plants but in spring, tulips, grape hyacinths and crocuses add splashes of colour to the sea of grass. In autumn, spiked speedwell appears and the songs of grasshoppers and bush crickets fill the air. Birds of the steppes include pallid harriers, rose-coloured starlings, several species of larks and waders and the immense great bustard.

You are not likely to see the saiga antelope outside nature reserves

Mammals such as sousliks and marmots live in underground burrows and are quite widespread, while the once endangered saiga antelope is still more or less restricted to reserves.

Outstanding areas of steppe can be seen in the Askania-Nova Reserve near the Black Sea and the Central Black-Earth (Tsentralno-Chernozomny) Reserve at Kursk.

Broad-Leaved Woodlands

Moscow lies in a transition zone between the hardy coniferous forests of northern Russia and the scrub and steppe habitat to the south. The typical natural vegetation of the region around the capital is mixed forest comprising scattered evergreen trees and a wide range of broad-leaved, deciduous species such as oak, beech, lime and birch. Although much of the native woodland has been cleared in the immediate vicinity of Moscow, mature parks and gardens in the suburbs often retain many woodland species and large tracts of prime forest can be found farther afield from the capital.

During the winter months the woodlands may appear bleak and austere, often giving the impression of being lifeless. Many of the birds have migrated to more favourable climates, while most of the invertebrates and some of the mammals pass the cold months in states of dormancy or torpor. However, wild boar, deer and foxes still have to forage for food, and

PEACE AND QUIET

great-spotted woodpeckers, lesser-spotted woodpeckers and flocks of tits forage for insects hidden among the twigs and bark.

Those smaller birds that do remain during the winter months generally move around in roving flocks, so visitors should patiently look and listen for their presence: initially there will be nothing in sight; then, all of a sudden, the trees will be full of birds as a flock moves through. After dark, tawny owls hunt for small mammals and their presence can be detected by the familiar 'kewick' call.

In spring, the woodland floor bursts into life with patches of wood sorrel, primroses and orchids playing host to a variety of insects, including butterflies such as orange tip, speckled wood and brimstone. By late summer, the shade cast by the leaf canopy is too dense to allow much light through to the ground below. Most ground-dwelling flowers therefore make use of light available in spring. Spring also heralds the arrival of migrant birds such as pied, spotted and red-breasted flycatchers, chiffchaffs, blackcaps, redstarts and cuckoos; on their arrival, they add to the chorus of bird song from the resident species. At ground level, mice and voles scurry among the fallen leaves

Silvery streaks of taiga trees: birch, poplar and pine

and red squirrels are more conspicuous at this time of year than at other seasons.

The Taiga

Taiga is the Russian name given to the great belt of coniferous forest that dominates the northern latitudes of the country. It stretches all the way from the Baltic coast to the Sea of Okhotsk. Spruce and fir trees dominate these woodlands, and these evergreen trees can tolerate some of the harshest winter weather. Not surprisingly, the taiga has been a rich source of timber for building and firewood, the evidence for this being most noticeable around towns and cities. However, in areas cleared of conifers, birch is quick to colonise and a mosaic woodland soon forms. The shade cast by dense stands of conifers is such that the ground flora is comparatively poor, although mosses, liverworts and ferns often thrive in the damp, still air. The birdlife of the taiga is noticeably different from that of the broad-leaved woodland. Beautifully marked hazelhens

Fungi

Fungi appear in the autumn and are more noticeable in birch woodland than under conifers. Many different shapes and colours can be found, including species of *Boletus* and fly agarics. Gathering edible fungi is a popular pastime for Russian residents. Several examples find their way to the markets where the more select species can command high prices.

nest and feed inconspicuously on the woodland floor, while black woodpeckers and white-backed woodpeckers excavate their own hole in the trunk of a tree. Ural owls and great-grey owls, on the other hand, use the fork of a tree or sometimes occupy an abandoned crow's nest. Both species of owl are large and will take quarry as large as capercaillie or a hare. Thrushes are also well represented in the taiga: blackbirds, redwings and fieldfares build neat nests of twigs and mosses in the forks of trees. Crossbills are widespread and small flocks form outside the breeding season. As their name suggests, the tips of the bill are crossed and are ideally suited to prising out the seeds from pine cones.

Many of the taiga's mammals have beautifully warm coats, helping them endure the winters. Regrettably, these also make them targets for the fur-trade and species like fox, wolf and sable are justifiably wary of man. The forests also harbour elk, or moose, and despite their massive size these creatures are surprisingly quiet and unobtrusive.

Tundra

The tundra is the most northerly vegetated zone in Russia, occupying an area beyond the forested taiga. To the north lies the frozen Arctic, a land of ice flows and shattered rock. Because of the northerly latitude it occupies, the tundra is necessarily difficult to reach, but the Kola peninsula is the most accessible area from St Petersburg. With the exception

PEACE AND QUIET

of prostrate forms of juniper, dwarf birch and dwarf willow, this is a treeless landscape, but one which is nevertheless botanically rich. Although blanketed by ice and snow in winter, mosses, clubmosses and lichens are abundant, and during the brief summer mountain avens, cowberry, crowberry, Arctic poppy, moss campion and saxifrages add colourful variety.

The marshy ground is home to millions of midges and also to large numbers of birds. Waders such as dotterel, spotted redshank, greenshank, golden plover, broad-billed sandpiper, red-necked phalarope and Temminck's stint and numerous wildfowl nest close to water, while ptarmigan, lapland buntings and snowy owls prefer more broken ground. The latter feeds mainly on lemmings and Arctic voles, which, in some years, can be abundant.

The Baltic Coast

After visiting the sights of Moscow and St Petersburg, a trip to the Baltic Coast or a cruise along the Gulf of Finland can make a refreshing change. The sea air is invigorating and the wide range of maritime species of bird, which are not found inland, adds variety to a trip to Russia.

During the summer months, undisturbed stretches of coast hold a number of breeding birds. Black guillemots and eider ducks nest on rocky coasts but spend a considerable amount of time feeding on the sea. Black guillemots catch fish, while eiders prefer mussels and other shellfish. Red-throated divers also fish on the open sea but nest beside inland pools. Together with black-throated divers, grebes and seaduck, their numbers build up during spring and autumn migration. Gulls are also very much a feature of the coast, the numbers and the variety of species changing with the seasons. Black-headed, common and little gulls are summer visitors, while many herring and great black-backed gulls remain throughout the year. Flocks should be checked in winter for more unusual species.

Belovezhskaya Pushcha Reserve

Belovezhskaya Pushcha lies on the western border of Russia and is contiguous with the world-famous Bialowieza Reserve in Poland. The primeval forests that comprise this remarkable area are among the most unspoilt in Europe, and are home to an amazing variety of plants and animals. The reserve provides an insight into what much of Europe must have looked like thousands of years ago. Compared to many areas in Europe, mammals are well

European Bison
Standing around 6 feet (1.8m) at the shoulder, the European Bison is arguably Russia's most imposing native mammal. Numbers have declined through a combination of hunting and habitat loss. Today they survive only in reserves where their numbers are slowly increasing.

represented in the reserve with wild boar, foxes, wolves, polecats, pine martens, dormice and harvest mice all being present. Most famous of all, however, is the population of European bison.

Broad-leaved trees, such as oak, hornbeam and alder, predominate in Belovezhskaya and, in turn, support many breeding birds.

Pondering his close shave...one of the European bison, rescued from extinction and living at the Belovezhskaya Pushcha Reserve

The Oka Reserve

The Oka Reserve lies in the Ryazan district, less than 100 miles (160km) to the east of Moscow, and is the capital's most accessible reserve. It is an area of varied habitats comprising mixed woodland, and elements of steppe, taiga and marshland vegetation, with the River Oka as its centrepiece.

European bison, which were introduced from Poland, and aurochs now breed here, and the woodlands harbour red

squirrels, roe deer, pine martens and numerous small mammals. White-tailed eagles, ospreys, black kites, kingfishers, otters and introduced beavers are found in the vicinity of the river and marshes, which support large numbers of frogs, toads and newts. The vegetation is rich and colourful and includes irises, fritillaries and marsh orchids, while in the more boggy areas sundews, bog myrtles and bilberries grow. Several species of woodpecker, including the immense black woodpecker, excavate nest holes in the larger tree trunks, and black storks and honey buzzards build nests of twigs and branches. In early spring warblers and flycatchers arrive and sing loudly to claim a territory.

The Darwin Reserve and Rybinsk Reservoir

Two hundred miles (320km) to the north of Moscow lies the immense Rybinsk Reservoir, which is situated on the transition zone between Russia's broad-leaved deciduous forests and the coniferous taiga further north. The Darwin Reserve, which borders the northern shores of the lake, mainly comprises large tracts of taiga with spruce and pine predominating, but variety is added to the area by marshes and bogs.

Open marshland is home to cranes which, despite their size, are extremely wary creatures ideally suited to the expansive terrain. Flowers such as cottongrass and sundew flourish in the marshlands, which also provide ideal nesting grounds

for teal, mallards, shovelers, curlew and wood sandpipers. All species keep a wary eye open for white-tailed eagles, which nest in the forests and prey upon unsuspecting birds and mammals.

Wolverines, wolves and brown bears live in the forest but are retiring species, only seen by chance, as are the nesting Ural and great-grey owls.

Travelling Farther Afield

Moscow and St Petersburg themselves can be exciting enough, but trips can sometimes be made farther afield to visit some of the more spectacular regions of mountains, deserts and inland seas. These normally need to be planned well in advance, and often mean joining an organised tour.

Lake Baikal is one of the more distant destinations, lying near the border with China in the foothills of the Transbaikalian Mountains. The lake has been land-locked for so long that many of its species are unique and found nowhere else in the world. It can even claim its own species of seal.

Nearer to Moscow, the Black Sea and Caspian Sea (the largest inland sea) offer aquatic life on a grand scale. The Caspian also has its own species of seal, and both have unique species of fish and huge breeding colonies of wetland birds around their margins. Less easy to visit but certainly unsurpassed in their mountainous splendour are the Caucasus Mountains, the Tien Shan Mountains and the Pamir Mountains of Uzbekistan.

Russian markets are worth exploring for the characters if not for the food itself!

FOOD AND DRINK

There has been a restaurant revolution in Moscow and St Petersburg over the last decade. Both cities now offer a wide variety of dining-out experiences: Moscow has many fast food outlets; in St Petersburg these are thinner on the ground. Prices are high even by Western standards but most restaurants offer good value for money and attentive service. Many places stay open until at least midnight, but if you are dining out bear in mind that the metro closes at 01.00hrs. English is usually found on menus and an increasing proportion of staff are familiar with European languages.

The most important element in a Russian meal is the *zakuski* or hors d'oeuvres. There may be a dozen dishes on the table as well as bottles of vodka and Russian champagne (a sweeter and lighter version of the French equivalent). It may be a couple of hours before the main course is started.

If you're not eating out, there are bars in all the major hotels, at least one of which will stay open into the small hours. Most bars serve snacks or even meals well into the evening at reasonable prices. Drinks however,

FOOD AND DRINK

especially in the cocktail lounges, are very expensive. Bars outside the hotels are scarce and largely confined to shopping malls and other large complexes.

Hors d'oeuvres
caviar (*ikra*; **икра**)
pancakes with caviar (*bliny s'ikroi*; **блины с икрой**)
pancakes with sour cream (*bliny so smetanoi*; **блины со сметаной**)
pickled mushrooms (*marinovaniye griby*; **маринованые грибы**)

smoked salmon (*kopchonaya syomga*; **копуеная семга**)

Dessert
apple pie (*yablochny pirog*; **яблочный пирог**)
ice cream (*morozhenoye*; **мороженое**)
rum baba (*romovaya baba*; **ромовая баба**)

Drinks
beer (*pivo*; **пиво**): sold in bottles and often of good quality.

A food and drink kiosk in Moscow

FOOD AND DRINK

brandy (*konyak*; **коньяк**): Armenian and Azerbaijani are highly recommended brands.
kvass (**квас**): a slightly alcoholic drink fermented from rye bread, popular in the summer.
vodka (**водка**): usually sold in measures of 100 grams. Common brands are Stolichnaya and Moskovskaya.
water (*voda*; **вода**): drink only bottled mineral water, not tap water.
wine (*vino*; **вино**): the best Russian wines are imported from Georgia, Moldavia or the Crimea. Wines from Bulgaria are also good. Try Tsinandali (dry white) or Mukuzani (dry red). For those with a sweet palate, try the wines from the Caucasus and the Crimea. You will also find champagne *(shampanskoye)* on most menus. Do not expect Moet et Chandon! Russian sparkling wines tend to be very sweet but very cheap and lie quite easily on the stomach. There is an excellent Georgian sparkling dry white wine called Chkhaveri.

Fish
fried pike-perch (*sudak fri*; **судак фри**)
herring (*syeld*; **сельдь**)
salmon (*syomga*: **семга**)
sturgeon in tomato sauce (*osetrina po-russki*; **осетрина по-русски**)
trout (*foryel*; **форель**)

Meat
beef Stroganoff (**ьэф-строганов**)
chicken Kiev (*kotlety po-kievski*; **котлеты ро-киевски**)
duck with apples (*utka s'yablokami*; **утка с яблоками**)

grilled steak (*bifshteks*; **бифштекс**)
kebabs (*shashlik*; **шашлык**)
pies (with a variety of fillings) (*pirogi*; **пирогы**)
pilau rice with mutton (*ploff iz baraniny*; **плов из баранины**)
roast pork with plums (*zharkoye iz svininy so slivami*; **жаркое из свинины со сливами**)

Soups
beetroot, cabbage and meat (*borshch*; **борш**)
cabbage and meat (*shchi*; **ши**)
cold vegetable (*okroshka*; **окрошка**)
meat or fish soup, flavoured with cucumber, tomatoes, olives, capers, lemon and sour cream (*solianka*; **солянка**)

Moscow

Restaurants and Cafés
Aleksandrovsky, 1-ya Tverskaya Yamskaya Ulitsa 17. Old Russian dishes with traditional gypsy entertainment.
Anchor, Tverskaya-Yamskaya Ulitsa 19. First-class sea food restaurant at the Palace Hotel.
Arbatskie Vorota, Arbat Ulitsa 11. Russian and European food in a central location.
Arkadia Traktir, Teatralniy Proezd 3. Russian and international cuisine to jazz accompaniment.
Aragvi, Tverskaya Ulitsa 6. Georgian cuisine: Sulguni cheese, spiced meat soup *(kharcho)*, roast sturgeon *(osetrina na vertelye)* and chicken tabaka. Georgian wines: Tsinandali, Mukuzani, Kakhetia.
Arlecchino, Druzhinnikovskaya Ulitsa 15. Quality Italian cooking and wines.

FOOD AND DRINK

Atrium, Leninskiy Prospekt 44. Russian and European cuisine in a classical setting.

Baku Livan, Tverskaya Ulitsa 24. Middle Eastern dishes, including more than 20 kinds of pilau *(ploff)*, sour milk and meat soup *(dovta)*, grilled sausage *(lyulys-kebab)*, stuffed vine leaves *(golubtsky)* and roast lamb with pomegranates *(nakurma)*. Wines: Matrassa, Shamkhor.

Chicken Grill, Sadko Arcade, Krasnogvardeyskiy Proezd 1. Grilled chicken to eat in or take away.

Guriya Café, Komsomlskiy Prospekt 7/3. Reliable Georgian cuisine.

Kashtan, Taganskaya Ulitsa 40/42. European and Caucasian cuisine with rowdy evening floor show.

Kolkhida, Sadovaya-Samotyochnaya 6. Georgian food in a pleasant setting.

Kropotkinskaya 36, Ulitsa Prechistenka 36. The first co-operative restaurant in the Soviet Union when it opened in 1987. Excellent Russian cuisine.

La Cantina, Tverskaya Ulitsa 5. Tex-Mex in a great location.

Les Champs Elysées, Korovinskoe Shosse 10. French cooking for gourmets at the Pullman Iris Hotel.

McDonalds, Ulitsa Arbat 50/52; Bolshaya Bronnaya Ulitsa 29; or Gazetniy Pereulok 6.

Panda, Tverskoy Bulvar 3/5. Authentic Chinese cuisine in downtown Moscow. Reservations advised.

Pizza Hut, Tverskaya Ulitsa 12; or Kutuzovskiy Prospekt 17. Dine in or take away.

Razgulyay, Spartakovskaya Ulitsa 11. A delightful cellar restaurant with traditional Russian cuisine and gypsy music at the weekend.

Rossiya Hotel (Russky Zal), Varvarka Ulitsa 6. High quality Russian cuisine. Try the *borshch* and the *blinys*.

Russkiy Traktir, Ulitsa Arbat 44. Russian cuisine in the Arbat.

Sapporo, Prospekt Mira 14. Sushi, Tempura and other authentic Japanese dishes.

Tren-Mos, Komsomolskiy Prospekt 21/10. Hamburgers and steaks, American-style.

U Pirosmani, Novodevichiy Proezd 4. Superb Georgian cuisine in this restaurant near the Novodevichiy Monastery.

U Yuzefa, Dubininskaya Ulitsa 11/17. Moscow's famous Jewish restaurant. Ethnic music.

Uzbekistan, Ulitsa Neglinnaya 29. Specialities include meat and noodle soup *(lagman)*, Scotch eggs *(tkhum-dulma)* and roast mutton ribs *(baranina kopeka)*. Uzbek wines.

Bars

Artists' Bar, Teatralniy Proezd 1/4. The sophisticated ambience of the Hotel Metropol, perfect for after-theatre supper or drinks.

Heineken Beer Bar, Hotel Kosmos, Prospekt Mira 150. Beer and snacks. Open 24 hours.

Hermitage Bar, Savoy Hotel, Rozhdestvenka Ulitsa 3. Classy turn-of-the-century bar in this up-market hotel.

Jacko's Bar, Ulitsa Kalanchevskaya 21/40. Blues, jazz and drinking till dawn at the Hotel Leningrad.

Lobby Bar, Radisson Slavjanskaya Hotel, Berezhkovskaya Naberezhanaya 2. Drink to the strains of string quartet or concert piano.

News Pub, Petrovka Ulitsa 18. Foreign newspapers as well as a wide selection of beer, cocktails and pub food.

Red Lion Pub, World Trade Centre, Krasnopresnenskaya naberezhnaya 12. 'Traditional' British pub. Open to midnight.

Remi's, Krasnogvardeyskiy Proezd 1. Piano bar in the Sadko Arcade.

Santa Lucia Bar, Hotel Intourist, Tverskaya Ulitsa 3/5. Drinks and snacks until midnight.

Dining out – a Russian way of life

Tex-Mex Bar, Khrustalniy Pereulok 1. Guacamole and chilli as well as live music, pool, darts and Mexican beer.

St Petersburg

Restaurants and Cafés

St Petersburg boasts a number of high quality restaurants and cafés, some of which are below:

Afrodita, Nevskiy Prospekt 86. Seventeen different cuisines including Italian and Spanish. Fish a speciality.

Austeria, Petropavlovskaya Krepost. An elegant restaurant in one of the bastions of the Peter-Paul Fortress.

FOOD AND DRINK

The Brasserie, Mikhaylovskaya Ulitsa 1/7. Elegant dining at the Grand Hotel Europe for just affordable prices.

Bristol, Nevskiy Prospekt 22. Centrally located café serving pizza and snacks.

Chayka, Ekaterininskaya Kanala naberezhanaya 14. Central café-bar, popular with the tourists.

Daddy's Steak Room, Moskovskiy Prospekt 73. 'The best steaks in St Petersburg'; also pizzas.

Dom Arkhitektora, Bolshaya Morskaya Ulitsa 52. Reservations required in this classic Russian restaurant.

Dr Oetker, Nevskiy Prospekt 40. Friendly pub-restaurant in a 19th-century confectioners.

Duke Konstantin, Millionaya Ulitsa 5/1. Italian cuisine in the beautiful setting of the Marble Palace.

Fortetsiya, Ulitsa Kuibysheva 7. Cosy restaurant not far from the St Petersburg Hotel.

Hebei, Bolshoy Prospekt 61 (Petrograd side).Chinese cooks prepare traditional dishes from Hebei province. Nearest metro Petrogradskaya.

Le Café, Nevskiy Prospekt 142. Despite the name, a German-run bakery and café at the upper end of Nevskiy.

Literary Café, Nevskiy Prospekt 18. Old-style café where Russian poet, Alexander Pushkin, once dined.

Pietari, Moskovskiy Prospekt 222. Moderately-priced restaurant with live music and dancing – opposite Pulkovskaya Hotel.

Pizza-House, Podolskaya Ulitsa 23. Eat in or take away – near Tekhnologichesiy Institut Metro.

Schwabski Domik, Krasnogvardeyskiy Prospeky 28/19. Schnitzel, wurst, German beer; the works.

Stroganov, Nevskiy Prospekt 17. Italian and Russian specialities in a formal setting.

Tbilisi, Sytninskaya Ulitsa 1/7. Friendly Georgian restaurant, popular with the locals.

Bars

Angleterre, Hotel Astoria, Bolshaya Morskaya Ulitsa 39. Carlsberg beer. Open to 2am.

Astoria Night Bar, Bolshaya Morskaya Ulitsa 39. Live music and dancing to 5am.

Beer Garden, Nevskiy Prospekt 86. Set back off the main street, the terrace is a haven for the weary sightseer.

John Bull, Nevskiy Prospekt 79. Traditional English pub, but open till 5am.

Joy, Lomonosova Ulitsa 1/28. Three bars, discotheque and casino.

Panorama Bar, Hotel Pribaltiyskaya, Korablestroiteley Ulitsa 14. Magnificent view of the Gulf of Finland in this popular tourist hotel.

Sadko's, Mikhaylovskaya Ulitsa 1/7. Classy rendezvous point located within the Grand Hotel Europe.

The Beer Stube, Nevskiy Prospekt 57. Drinks including non-alcoholic beer in the Nevskij Palace Hotel.

Warsteiner Forum, Nevskiy Prospekt 120. Traditional German Bierstube – metro Ploshchad Vosstaniya.

White Nights Bar, Hotel Olympia, Morskoy Slavy Ploshchad. Open mid-May to mid-September only.

SHOPPING

Don't be shy about having a look around Russian shops even if you don't want to buy anything. Prices are always marked in roubles. To make a purchase, choose what you want and ask or signal to the assistant to write down the price, then queue at a cash desk (*kassa*; **касса**) to pay. Finally, return to the counter with your receipt and collect your purchase. Opening hours are around 09.00–19.00hrs (some department stores open at 10.00hrs but stay open until 21.00hrs). Closed Sundays (except some larger stores in the city centre).

Some ideas for presents:
Vodka: the prices may seem steep but look for quality brands, which are not usually on sale in the West. Never buy from kiosks – the prices may be tempting but goods can be contaminated and counterfiet. The best known Russian brands are Stolichnaya, Moskovskaya, Russkaya and Pshenichnaya; also look out for the more expensive Pyotr Veliki.

Colourful costumes sported by ranks of Russian dolls

SHOPPING

Flavoured vodkas are frowned on by Russians but are popular with tourists. Try limonaya or the more exotic okhotnichaya (a mixture of cloves, ginger and juniper berries).

Palekh boxes: hand-painted and lacquered by local craftsmen, some from the village of Palekh near Moscow.

Matrioshka: the famous Russian nesting dolls.

Records and cassettes: very cheap and perfectly playable but of inferior technical quality to those available in the West. Go for Russian music.

Balalaikas: traditional Russian stringed instrument.

Books: the glossy art books produced by the museums are often reasonably priced and you may even pick up a bargain. Never buy a book from a street vendor, however, without inspecting it first as picture reproduction is often poor.

Moscow

Department Stores and Shopping Malls

GUM, Krasnaya Ploshchad 3. Mainly western outlets including Bennetton, Estée Lauder, Galeries Lafayette, Phillips, Sony, Kodak, as well as cafés and restaurants.

Olympic Supermarket, Krasnaya Presnya Ulitsa 23. Food, drink, clothes, toys and cosmetics.

Petrovskiy Passazh, Petrovka Ulitsa 10. Leading Western brand names as well as up-market Russian clothing outlets.

Sadko Arcade, Krasnogvardeyskiy Proezd 1. Western outlets including a wide variety of eateries.

TsUM (Central Department Store), Petrovka Ulitsa 2. Traditional Russian store.

Food Shops

Deila Food Store and Delicatessen, Ostozhenka Ulitsa 35. A range of imported foods, sausage, cheese and spirits.

Gastronom Novoarbatskiy, Novy Arbat Ulitsa 13. Russia's biggest supermarket.

SIAG, Tversakaya Ulitsa 22. Groceries, sweets and spirits.

Gift Shops

Church of St George, Varvarka Ulitsa 12. Beautiful crafts, produced by local artists. Token admission charge.

Kupina, Novy Arbat Ulitsa 8. Large selection of traditional Russian souvenirs in the main bookshop (Dom Knigi).

Russkiy Suvenir, Kutuzovskiy Prospekt 9. Lacquer boxes and other traditional souvenirs.

Suveniry, Ulitsa Arbat 23. Matryoshkas, china, crystal etc.

Books, Records and CD's

Melodiya, Novy Arbat Ulitsa 22. The old state record store sells CD's, tapes and video cassettes.

Moskovskiy Dom Knigi, Noviy Arbat Ulitsa 8. Some foreign language books.

Rhapsody Music Store, Myasnitskaya Ulitsa 17. A wide range of CD's, records, audio and video cassettes.

Zwemmer's, Kuznetskiy Most Ulitsa 18. Unbeatable source of foreign books in English – some Russian books too.

Markets

Izmaylovskiy Park, Narodniy Prospekt 17. Art market, flea market and souvenirs, well worth a visit.

Shopping on Nevskiy Prospekt

St Petersburg

Department Stores and Shopping Malls

The Nevskiy Prospekt – the lower end of St Petersburg's premier street is devoted to shopping and commerce, especially Western cosmetics and other up-market items. **Apraksin Dvor**, Sadovaya Ulitsa. A row of small shops facing the street conceals several rows of market outlets inside the courtyard. Colourful, but beware of pick-pockets.

SHOPPING

Babylon Super, Maliy Prospekt 54–56 (Petrograd Side). One stop shopping with excellent food and wine department.
Gostiniy Dvor, Nevskiy Prospekt 35. St Petersburg's most famous shopping mall has been closed for refurbishment for some time.
Passazh, Nevskiy Prospekt 48. Upmarket mall/department store with many Western fashion shops, accessories, electronics, cosmetics and jewellery.

Food Shops

Babylon Mini Market, Nevskiy Prospekt 69. Food, snacks and drinks including imported wine and liquors.
Eliseevskiy, Nevskiy Prospekt 56. Still named after its 19th-century proprietor, this is St Petersburg's best known food hall – the décor has to be seen to be believed.
Kalinka Stockmann, Finlandskiy Prospekt 1. Comprehensive Western-owned supermarket, located just behind Hotel St Petersburg.
Nevskiy Delicatessen, Nevskiy Prospekt 71/Marata Ulitsa 1. Meat, fish, pizza, cakes and pastries, fruit and vegetables.

Gift Shops

Marble Palace, Millionnaya Ulitsa 5/1. Fine Russian gifts by individual artists.
Nasledie, Nevskiy Prospekt 116. High up on the avenue, this is one of the best of the traditional Russian gift shops.
Serebryanye Ryady, Dumskaya Ulitsa 1. 'Silver Row' gifts and souvenirs.
Suveniry, Nevskiy Prospekt 92. Russian souvenirs.

Books, Records and CD's

Dom Knigi, Nevskiy Prospekt 28. The largest book shop in St Petersburg, including limited selection of books in English.

Honey-sellers at Kuznechny market

The elegant, shining curve of the Cosmos, one of Moscow's major hotels, built by the French for the 1980 Olympics

Melodiya, Nevskiy Prospekt 32/4. Old Soviet record store, also sells cassettes, CD's and books.

The Hermitage Gallery produces its own range of books devoted to its art treasures.

Markets

Kuznechny Rynok, Kuznechny Pereulok 3. The most accessible of St Petersburg's farmers' markets is definitely worth a visit. Closed second Tuesday. Nearest metro Vladimirskaya.

Sennaya Ploshchad, the setting for much of Dostoyevsky's novel *Crime and Punishment*, is the Haymarket today and a centre for Russia's famous (or infamous) street kiosks.

ACCOMMODATION

The hotel situation in both cities is improving all the time but there is still a dearth of accommodation in the budget category. Some Soviet-era hotels are currently being renovated and upgraded and may offer the best bargain although they tend to be over-large and lacking atmosphere. An increasing number of tourist hotels are operated as joint-

ACCOMMODATION

ventures with a foreign hotel management company – a reliable indicator of Western standards of accommodation and service. Don't rely on Russian hotel ratings.

When choosing a hotel in St Petersburg, bear in mind that the metro system is far less extensive here than in Moscow. Some Russian-run hotels still retain the *dezhurnaya* or floor attendant.

Whenever you leave the hotel, hand your key to the *dezhurnaya*, she will give it back to you when you return. The *dezhurnaya* is the person to complain to about broken light bulbs, lack of toilet paper, or other inconveniences.

Moscow Hotels

Art Hotel, Prospekt Vernadskovo 41 (tel: 432 7827; Metro: Prospekt Vernadskovo). Opened 1994, this small

One of Europe's biggest hotels: the Rossiya, which can take 6,000 guests

German-run establishment claims to be the first middle-class hotel in Moscow.

Baltchug Kempinski, Baltchug Ulitsa 1 (tel: 230 6500; Metro: Novokuznetskaya). First-class hotel, convenient for the Tretyakov picture gallery.

Cosmos, Prospekt Mira 150 (tel: 217 0785; Metro: VVTs). Built by the French for the Moscow Olympics in 1980 (more than 1,700 rooms); far out from central Moscow.

Danilovskiy, Bolshoy Starodanilovskiy Pereulok 5 (tel: 954 0503; Metro: Tulskaya). Modern hotel with good facilities including swimming pool, restaurant and bar.

Intourist, Tverskaya Ulitsa 3–5 (tel: 956 4426; Metro: Teatralnaya).

Metropole, Teatralny Proezd 14 (tel: 927 6000; Metro: Teatralnaya). Designed by a British architect, W Walcott. Moscow's premier hotel is well worth a look around, even if you're not lucky enough to be staying there yourself.

Moscow Travellers Guest House, Ulitsa Bolshaya Pereyaslavskaya 50, floor 10 (tel: 971 4059; Metro: Prospekt Mira). Recently-opened youth hostel under American auspices. Book early.

National, Okhotny Ryad, near Red Square (tel: 258 7000; Metro: Teatralnaya). Newly-refurbished. Lenin stayed here for a while when the Soviet Government moved to Moscow from Petrograd early in 1918.

Palace Hotel, 1-ya Tverskaya Yamskaya Ulitsa 19 (tel: 956 3152; Metro: Belorusskaya). A Marco Polo (Austrian) hotel;

small establishment with excellent standards.

President Hotel, Bolshaya Yakimanka Ulitsa 24 (tel: 238 7303; Metro: Oktyabrskaya). Once patronised by Communist Party big-wigs, good location for Gorky Park.

Radisson Slavjanskaya, Berezhkovskaya naberzhnaya 2 (tel: 941 8020; Metro: Kievskaya). Deluxe, American-run hotel with 430 rooms and excellent facilities including shopping arcade and business centre.

Rossiya, Varvarka Ulitsa 6 (tel: 298 5531), which has more than 3,000 rooms and is one of the largest hotels in Europe. You will find it just behind Red Square – you can't miss it! (Metro: Kitai Gorod).

Savoy Hotel, Ulitsa Rozhdestvenka 3 (tel: 929 8555; Metro: Lubyanka). A top grade hotel in an excellent location.

Ukrain, Kutuzovskiy Prospekt 2 (tel: 243 2895; Metro: Kievskaya). Overlooks the Moscow River. Excellent value.

St Petersburg Hotels

Astoria, Bolshaya Morskaya Ulitsa 39 (tel: 210 5032; Metro: Nevskiy Prospekt). Centrally situated, luxury hotel, with an atmosphere reminiscent of old St Petersburg.

Grand Hotel Europe, Mikhaylovskaya Ulitsa 1/7 (tel: 119 6000; Metro: Gostiny Dvor). St Petersburg's most prestigious hotel, beautifully restored and in an ideal location.

Mir, Gastello Ulitsa 17 (tel: 108 5166; Metro: Moskovskaya). Good value, but not central.

Nevskij Palace, Nevskiy Prospekt 57 (tel: 311 6366;

Metro: Mayakovskaya).
Nineteenth-century building,
recently restored to five-star
standard.
Oktyabrskaya Hotel, Ligovskiy
Prospekt 10 (tel: 277 6012;
Metro: Ploshchad Vosstaniya).
Former Soviet hotel, opposite
Moscow railway station.
Olympia, Ploshchad Morskoy
Slavy (tel: 119 6800). New hotel
near the passenger sea terminal.
Bar and restaurant. Good value.
Pribaltiyskaya, Ulitsa
Korablestroitelei 14 (tel: 356

*Looming over the Moskva (Moscow)
River, the stately Ukrain Hotel has a
distinctive outline*

0001; Metro: Primorskaya). A
modern, Swedish-built hotel
close to the port. Too large and
impersonal for some tastes but
facilities include six bars/snack
bars, saunas, swimming pool,
bowling-alley and souvenir shop.
Pulkovskaya, Ploshchad
Pobedy 1 (tel: 264 5122; Metro:
Moskovskaya). Finnish-built
hotel with all the mod cons.

Rus Hotel, Artilleriyskaya Ulitsa 1 (tel: 279 5003; Metro: Chernyshevskaya). Modern Russian-Italian joint venture with the usual facilities.

St Petersburg, Vyborgskaya Naberezhnaya 5/2 (Metro: Ploshchad Lenina). A luxurious hotel with excellent facilities. Opposite the Cruiser *Aurora* (now closed for refurbishment).

St Petersburg International Hostel, 3-ya Rozhdestvenskaya Ulitsa 28 (tel: 277 0569; Metro: Ploshchad Vosstaniya). An American venture aimed at youngsters and back-packers.

Nightclubs are appearing fast to cater for Russia's new jet set

CULTURE, ENTERTAINMENT, NIGHTLIFE

The best way to let your hair down in Russia is to spend the evening in one of the city's livelier restaurants (see pages 85–8). This is where you are most likely to see ordinary Russians enjoying themselves. Restaurants generally stay open until midnight and you can take as long as you like over your meal. Many also have dance bands and/or a floor show, so you will be fully entertained. However, the better ones are in great demand so to make sure of a table, it is advisable to book.

CULTURE, ENTERTAINMENT, NIGHTLIFE

If you want to have a drink and chat into the early hours you will have to stay in the restaurants and hotels – Russia still lacks a bar or café culture, although there are signs that this is beginning to change. If you do decide to drink late though, don't forget that the Metro begins running down at about half past midnight.

There are plenty of nightclubs in Moscow and St Petersburg, but you should be careful in your choice as some clubs draw a shady clientele.

Moscow

Opera, Theatre and Ballet

You certainly will not want to leave Russia without sampling at least one of the cultural offerings for which the country is justly famous. Tickets for most productions are hard to come by, so as soon as you have settled in, find out what's on from your tour company or

It's worth making the effort to see a production at the Mariinskiy Theatre in St Petersburg: it has been associated with many great names

travel representative and book through them. Nowadays, you can expect to pay something more akin to the going Western rate for a performance, rather than the face value of the tickets. Before you go off at the deep end, remember that, being a foreigner, you stand a much greater chance of getting to a performance than the average Russian citizen – as you will appreciate when you see the forlorn figures milling about the theatre forecourt in search of unwanted tickets (culture is taken seriously here).

Most visitors want to spend an evening at the **Bolshoi Theatre** on Teatralnaya Ploshchad (tel: 292 0050). If the ballet or opera companies are not performing here, the alternative venue is the **Palace of Congresses** within the Kremlin.

Symphony Concerts and Recitals

Performed at the **Tchaikovsky Hall** on Triumalnaya Ploshchad 4/31 (tel: 299 5362; Metro: Mayakovskaya). Concerts also take place at the **Conservatory Grand Hall**, Bolshaya Nikitskaya Ulitsa 13 (tel: 229 8183; Metro: Biblioteka imeni Lenina); **Gnesin Russian Music Academy**, Malaya Rzhevskiy Pereulok 1 (tel; 290 6737; Metro: Arbatskaya); and **Oktyabr Concert Hall**, Ulitsa Novy Arbat 24 (tel: 291 2263; Metro: Arbatskaya).

Theatre

The **Moscow Art Theatre** (MKhAT), famous for its associations with Chekhov and Stanislavsky, is at Kamergerskiy Pereulok 3 (tel: 229 8760; Metro: Tverskaya). Other theatres include the **Maly**, on Teatralnaya Ploshchad 1/6 (tel: 924 4083; Metro: Nevskiy Prospekt); the **Moscow Drama Theatre**, known sometimes as Malaya Bronnaya from its location on Ulitsa Malaya Bronnaya 4 (tel: 290 4093); and the **Taganka Theatre**, Zemlyanoy Val Ploshchad 76 (tel: 271 2825).

Nightlife

Arbat Blues Club, Filippovskiy Pereulik 11 (tel: 291 1546). Blues and booze, smoky atmosphere.
Arkadia Jazz Club, Teatralniy Proezd 3 (tel: 926 9008). Jazz after midnight in the Arkadia restaurant.
Bunkr Music Club, Trifonovskaya Ulitsa 56 (tel: 284 3578). Live rock music in a basement near Rizhskaya metro.
Hermitage, Karetniy Ryad Ulitsa 3, (tel: 299 9774). Claims to cater for Bohemian types. In the Hermitage Gardens.
Manhatten Express, Varvarka Ulitsa 6 (tel: 298 5355). New nightclub and discotheque in the Hotel Rossiya.
Moskva Hill Night Club, Trubnaya Ploshchad 4 (tel: 208 3341). Variety show, bar and dancing.
Night Flight, Tverskaya Ulitsa 17 (tel: 299 4165). Western-style discotheque, expensive and you may need to show your passport.
Pilot, Trekhgorniy Val 6 (tel: 255 1552). Nightclub open Thursday to Saturday.

Circus

The world famous **Moscow State Circus** performs at Prospekt Vernadskovo 7 (new) and Svetnoy Bulvar (old). Nowadays, the packaging is as much variety show as traditional circus and many foreigners find the acts disappointing. During the summer there are tent circuses in **Gorky Park** and **Izmailovskiy Park**.

St Petersburg

Opera, Theatre and Ballet
St Petersburg has a vibrant and varied cultural life which is well worth exploring. The main theatres are:
Kirov Theatre of Opera and Ballet, Teatralnaya Ploshchad (tel: 114 4344; Metro: Sadovaya). Better known now by its pre-revolutionary name as the Mariinskiy. Some of Tchaikovsky's most famous ballets (including *Sleeping Beauty* and *The Nutcracker*) were premiered here and the great Russian bass, Chaliapin, regularly trod the boards.
Maly Theatre of Opera and Ballet, Ploshchad Isskustv 1 (tel: 219 1978; Metro: Nevskiy Prospekt). The Russian name means 'small' but the Maly Theatre can actually accommodate 1,200 people.
Pushkin Theatre, Aleksandriyskaya Ploshchad 2 (tel: 311 6139; Metro: Gostiniy Dvor).

Concerts
Bolshoy Philharmonic Hall, Mikhailovskiy Ulitsa 2 (tel: 110 4290; Metro: Nevskiy Prospekt).
Glinka Kapella Hall, Naberezhnaya Reki Moiki 20. The Glinka choir was founded by Peter the Great in 1713. Its standards are excellent and the concerts are well worth attending.
Maliy Zal of the Philharmonia, Nevskiy Prospekt 30 (tel: 312 4585; Metro: Nevskiy Prospekt).
Oktyabrskiy Concert Hall, Ligovskiy Prospekt 6 (tel: 277 6960; Metro: Ploshchad Vosstaniya).
Smolniy Cathedral Concert Hall, Rastrelli Ploshchad 3/1 (tel: 311 3560; Metro: Chernyshevskaya).

Nightlife
A O Troika, Zagorodniy Prospekt 27 (tel: 113 5343). Variety show in what claims to be the 'Moulin Rouge of St Petersburg'.
Eldorado, Tukhachevskovo Ulitsa 27/2 (tel: 226 3110). Bar, disco, dance show and casino in Hotel Karelia.
Hotelship Peterhof, Naberezhnaya Makarova (tel: 213 6321). Formal dinner dancing on a ship moored near the Tuchkov Bridge.
Joy, Lomonosova Ulitsa 1/28 (tel: 311 3540). Western-style disco near the Nevskiy Prospekt.
Nevskiy Melody, Sverdlovskaya Naberezhnaya 62 (tel: 227 1596). Restaurant, disco and casino.
Rock Around the Clock, Sadovaya Ulitsa 27 (tel: 310 0237). Live bands and enthusiastic crowd.
Rock-Club, Rubinshteyna Ulitsa 13 (tel: 312 3483). Live bands and information on local rock scene.
Star Dust, Aleksandrovskiy Park 4 (tel: 233 2712). Live music and disco situated near the Gorkovskaya Metro.

Winter in Russia is bitterly cold, but it is also spectacularly beautiful: the snow-capped Trinity Monastery of St Sergius in Sergievo Posad

Circus
The St Petersburg State Circus, Naberezhnaya Reki Fontanki 3. Summer performances held at **Shapito (Big Top) Summer Circus**, Avtovskaya Ulitsa 1a (tel: 314 1159; Metro: Gostiniy Dvor).

WEATHER AND WHEN TO GO

Moscow
You can enjoy Moscow any time of year. The weather is wonderfully invigorating in winter but also *very* cold (temperatures well below freezing are by no means uncommon any time from December to February). Snow

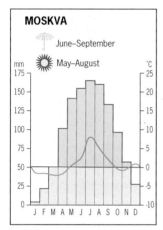

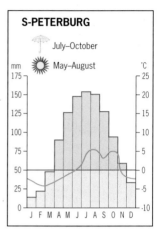

begins to fall during November, with the thaw starting in March, so if you dislike rain and slush avoid this period. In contrast, the summer months of June, July and August tend to be very hot, with temperatures rising to 85°–95°F (30°–35°C) in August. .

What to Wear

Winter: a warm winter coat covering the upper part of your legs is essential; a warm pair of trousers (jeans are not ideal in the depths of winter). You will also need a Russian-style fur hat or *shlyapka,* complete with ear muffs (a bobble or ski hat will not be enough), and a well-lined pair of gloves, a scarf and a sturdy pair of shoes or boots with skid-resistant soles. You do *not* need to worry about feeling cold indoors; Russian central heating systems are remarkably efficient. Summer: dress as you would in any West European country, but remember to pack a raincoat and umbrella. Take your swimming things, too.

St Petersburg

Generally, the climate is similar to Moscow. St Petersburg tends to be a few degrees warmer during winter but it often *feels* colder, because of the icy winds which whip across the Neva. In summer, on the other hand, the climate is just about ideal – warm but not too hot. For tourists lucky enough to be in the city during the latter part of June, the famous White Nights are a magical bonus.

HOW TO BE A LOCAL

The Russians are an open, generous and emotional people. They appreciate politeness, so try to learn the words for 'please', 'thank you' and 'excuse me' before you arrive. You may well arouse curiosity on the Metro, particularly if you are in a group. Do not be surprised if you are stared at from time to time; older Russians still find Western dress and behaviour somewhat extrovert. Russians are at their best in the more relaxed surroundings of bars and restaurants and you may well be invited over to their table or asked to dance. They will be offended if you turn them down. If you happen to be travelling on the Red Arrow (the night train which runs between Moscow and St Petersburg) you may find yourself sharing a sleeping compartment with a Russian couple! In these situations, formal introductions and handshakes are the norm. Don't wait to be asked to offer your seat to an elderly person and never put your feet on the seats (in Russia this is considered a particularly rude act).

Night becomes day during St Petersburg's White Nights; nighttime views such as this one of the River Moika can be disconcertingly bright!

You can't get a more Russian experience than the baths. Men and women bathe separately and usually on different days so no costumes are necessary. Bring your own towel, shampoo and plastic shoes or sandles. After paying a small admission charge and handing your valuables to the attendant, you will be given a plastic robe and offered a *venik* (a bundle of birch twigs), used to stimulate circulation. When using the sauna it is advisable to start on the lowest of the raised benches where the air is cooler. Alternate periods in the sauna with a dip in the pool. In Moscow, try the Sandunovskie Bani, Neglinnaya Ulitsa 14, open Wednesday to Monday 08.00–22.00hrs; and in St Petersburg, Banya, Olgi Forsh Ulitsa 6, open Wednesday to Sunday 08.00–22.00hrs.

PERSONAL PRIORITIES

Work on the assumption that you will be unable to find any of the following items in Russia and that it is therefore essential to bring adequate supplies with you: any medication, can opener, mosquito repellent, plastic shopping bags, photocopies of travel documents, nappies, creams and everything for baby; tampons or sanitary towels, male and female contraceptives, deodorants, toilet paper, etc.

Personal Safety

Some points to remember: never enter a taxi when there's already someone else inside. It's best to hire cabs from the hotel, rather than on the street and it doesn't cost any more. Apart from the main thoroughfares, Russian streets are poorly lit at night, so avoid side streets if you can. Always keep cameras, purses etc out of sight and don't loiter outside cafés and restaurants, it's a temptation to muggers. Be polite but firm when dealing with street traders if you don't intend to buy and walk straight on – don't allow yourself to be surrounded. And remember that the bars of the larger hotels are favourite pick-up points for Russian prostitutes so women are best advised not to drink alone.

CHILDREN

Moscow

Russian cities are not particularly well suited to the needs and interests of children. However, here are some ideas you might like to try:

The Circus: book through your hotel. If you are unlucky and the world famous Moscow State Circus is on tour, the reserve team will be playing in Gorky Park.

Ice Shows: the Moscow Ice Ballet performs at the Lenin Stadium, Sparrow Hills. Check with your hotel desk for up-to-date information.

The Zoo: Bolshaya Gruzinskaya Ulitsa 1 (Metro: Krasnopresnenskaya). Opening hours: 09.00–19.00hrs daily.

Swimming, **Skating**, **etc**: see **Sport**.

Theatre for Children: the Obraztsov Puppet Theatre at 3 Sadovaya-Samotyochnaya Ulitsa (tel: 299 5373) is well worth a visit; likewise, the **Moscow City Puppet Theatre**, Spartakovskaya Ulitsa 26 (tel: 261 2197) and the Children's Music Theatre, Vernadskovo Ulitsa 5 (tel: 930 7021). If you are interested in mime, try the Mime Theatre at Izmailovskiy Boulevard 41 (tel: 163 8150).

Parks: there are several major Moscow parks, with the usual recreational facilities (cafés, restaurants and so on). Gorky Park (Metro: Park Kultury), Sokolniki Park (Metro: Sokolniki) and Izmailovo Park (Metro: Izmailovskaya) are all well worth visiting. Gorky Park is the most popular with Muscovites and has an amusement area with boating lake, fun fair, fountains and open-air theatre, among other delights. Alternatively, you can watch the skating in winter.

River Cruises: if you are in Moscow between June and

September/October, why not take your children for a cruise on the Moscow river? The boat departs from the jetty near the Kiev Railway Station (Metro: Kievskaya).

A Matrioshka, or nesting doll, can provide one 'mother' or a whole family, according to your wishes

Food and Drink: Moscow in particular is well provided with fast food outlets like McDonalds and Pizza Hut which are run on identical lines to those in the West. The large shopping malls have cafés suitable for children (or you might like to try Buratino (Pinnochio) on Ulitsa Arbat). You can also buy ice cream from

CHILDREN

outlets in the shopping centres or try Baskin-Robbins at Arbat Ulitsa 20. Never buy food or drink from kiosks.

A trip on the St Petersburg Harbour Ferry is a treat for children and adults alike, and makes a change from trudging the streets

Places of Interest: Tsar's Bell and Cannon in the Kremlin, St Basil's Cathedral, the Tolstoy Estate, Ulitsa Lva Tolstovo, Polytechnical (Science) Museum, Novaya Ploshchad 3/4, the Armed Forces Museum (tanks etc) at Sovetskoy Armii Ulitsa 2.

St Petersburg

The St Petersburg Circus, Naberezhnaya Reki Fontanka 3. A must if you have been unable to get to the Moscow State Circus. Book as soon as you arrive.

The Zoo, Alexandrovskiy Park 1 (tel: 232 2839; Metro: Gorkovskaya). Open daily 10.00–20.00hrs.

Swimming, **Skating**, **etc**: see **Sport**.

Theatre for Children: Puppet and marionettes Theatre, Nevskiy Prospekt 52 (tel: 311 1900); Puppet Theatre,

Moskovskiy Prospekt 121 (tel: 298 0031).

Parks: the Kirov Park on Yelagin Island has the best recreational facilities in St Petersburg. Or you might try the Moskovskiy Park Pobedy, Kuznetsovskoy Ulitsa (Metro: Park Pobedy). Park Babushkina, Obukhovskoy Oborony Prospekt 149 (Metro: Lomonsovskaya).

River Cruises: available in the summer. Boats leave from the pier by the Winter Palace and from the Anichkov Bridge on Nevskiy Prospekt.

Food and Drink: never buy food or drink from kiosks. American ice cream can be bought at Baskin-Robbins, Nevskiy Prospekt 79.

Places of Interest: the Winter Palace, the Cruiser *Aurora*, the cells in the Peter-Paul Fortress, the Artillery Museum (tanks etc) in Alexandrovskiy Park, Peter the Great's Cabin, the Historical Waxworks in Kshesinskaya Mansion on Kuybysheva Ulitsa, the Railway Museum (free) at Sadovaya Ulitsa 50.

TIGHT BUDGET

Unless you are visiting Russia on a youth or student exchange, the package tour is still the best value for money you are likely to find. Cheap Russian hotels should be avoided unless recommended by someone you know. There are one or two youth hostels only, so make sure you book in advance. Buy your lunch from McDonalds or Pizza Hut, but avoid the stand-up snack bars and kiosks. Whenever possible, wander around on your own and avoid the tour guides – that way you will save money *and* learn a lot more about what makes the Russians tick. If your feet get tired pounding the pavement, jump on a bus or take the Metro; it's still extremely cheap. Museum charges are also very reasonable, once you have dispensed with the guided tour, so take your travel guide with you instead.

SPECIAL EVENTS

1 January: New Year's Day

7 January: Russian Orthodox Christmas

February–March: 'Farewell to the Russian Winter' folklore festival

8 March: International Women's Day

March or April: Russian Orthodox Easter, celebrated one week later than in the West

1 and 2 May: Labour Day/Spring Holiday

9 May: Victory Day (1945)

12 June: Russian Independence Day. A concerted effort is being made to make the most of this latest public holiday. Look out for events in major squares and parks

21 to 29 June: St Petersburg 'White Nights' Festival. It's twilight throughout the night during this period – look out for special events in hotels etc, but the best place to be is on the river

7 November: Formerly the anniversary of the Revolution and still a public holiday

25 December: Beginning of 'Russian Winter' Festival: a secular celebration involving family parties, concerts, New

Year trees, fireworks and Grandfather Frost – the Russian Father Christmas.
Nowadays Christmas is also celebrated by Christians again and there are major services in all churches.

SPORT

Moscow
Cross-Country Skiing: available at several locations in or just outside Moscow including Bittsevskiy Lesopark, Varshavskoe Shosse 143. Skis available from the Equestrian Centre.
Horse Racing and Cycling: these take place at the Hippodrome, Ulitsa Begovaya 22 (tel: 945 4367 for information in English). There is trotting and horse racing on Wednesday, Friday, Saturday and Sunday.
Horse Riding: Professional riding lessons are available at Bittsa Equestrian Centre, Balaklavskiy Prospekt 33.
Ice Hockey: the two Moscow football clubs, Dynamo and Central Army Club, play ice hockey in winter.
Ice Skating: there are skating rinks in winter at the Gorky and Sokolniki Parks (open 10.00–22.00hrs). Ask about hiring skates.
Soccer: the Russian football season runs from spring to autumn. Teams usually play on Saturday afternoons. Tickets may be obtained from Intourist or your hotel. The major venues are Dynamo Stadium, 36 Leningradskiy Prospekt and Army Palace of Sports, 39 Leningradskiy Prospekt. Important matches (including

internationals) may also take place at the Lenin Stadium/Palace of Sports at Luzhniki (Sparrow Hills).
Swimming: there are swimming pools in all the major hotels, including Intourist, Cosmos, Rossiya and Mezhdunarodnaya. (Swimming is not recommended in Russian pools.) In the summer you can go swimming at the beach in Seryebryany Bor on the Moskva River (Metro: Polezhaevskaya and trolleybuses: 20, 21 and 65).
Tennis: there are outdoor courts at most sports venues including Druzhba in Luzhniki Park (Metro: Sportivnaya).

St Petersburg
Cycling: Burevestrik Cycling Club, Engels Prospekt 81.
Cross-Country Skiing: there is a centre at Olgino on the Gulf of Finland.
Skating: there is an indoor rink at the Yubileyniy Palace of Sports, Dobrolyubova Ulitsa 18 (tel: 238 4061). Skates can be rented. There is an open-air skating rink for children at the Central Recreation Park, Tavricheskiy Sad.
Soccer, Hockey and other Spectator Sports: the major venues are Kirov Stadium, Krestovskiy Island, Petrovskiy Stadium, Petrovskiy Island, Jubilee Sports Palace, Dobrolyubova Prospekt, and Winter (Zimniy) Stadium, Manezhnaya Ploshchad 2. For tickets and further information, see the information desk at your hotel.
Swimming: use the small swimming pools in the major hotels.

DIRECTORY

A view of Red Square in Moscow

DIRECTORY

Arriving

Travel Documents: all visitors to Russia must have a visa as well as a passport. The most common type of visa is Tourist; your travel agent will issue you with the necessary application form which must be accompanied by three passport-sized photographs and photocopies of the first six pages of your passport. If you are an independent or business traveller, consult the Russian Embassy. Always allow several weeks for the processing of visas.

By air: the easiest way to get to Moscow and St Petersburg is to fly. Most major airlines fly to Moscow's international airport, Sheremetevo-2, and Pulkovo-2 in St Petersburg. You are strongly advised to travel on a foreign carrier – the Russian airline Aeroflot has aroused major concerns over safety. Procedures on arrival are standard; however visa and baggage checks are still laborious so expect a wait of at least one hour.

Facilities at the airports still fall short of Western standards. Services at Sheremetevo include post office, currency exchange, ticket sales, modest café and restaurant facilities and several small shops selling flowers, pharmaceuticals, duty-free goods, newspapers and souvenirs. Pulkovo is smaller but the facilities are similar – the duty-free services are better than in Moscow.

Sheremetevo is 19 miles (30km) northwest of Moscow and transport to the city centre is by coach or taxi. Pulkovo airport is 10 miles (17km) south of St Petersburg – a taxi ride takes about half-an-hour but there are also buses.

Sheremetevo Passenger Terminal, international arrivals (tel: 578 7518); departures (tel: 578 7816). Pulkovo Passenger Terminal, international arrivals and departures (tel: 104 3444).

By rail to Moscow: there are two routes to choose from. The first, via Ostend, Aachen, Hannover, Berlin, Warsaw and Brest leaves from London's Victoria Station; the second, via the Hook of Holland, leaves from London Liverpool Street. The journey time is usually about two-and-a-half days.

Train services operate in summer and winter but schedules vary. Sleeper-car reservations are obligatory on trains to Moscow and should be booked at least six weeks prior to departure. Most trains arrive at the Belorusskiy Voksal (Metro: Belorusskaya).

By rail to St Petersburg: there is a daily service from Paris, via Cologne, Hanover, Berlin and Warsaw. Trains arrive at Varshavskiy Voksal, Obvodnovo Kanala Naberezhnaya (Metro: Baltiyskaya).

By road: You will need a good working knowledge of Russian in order to follow road signs, buy petrol and, if necessary, cope with a breakdown. Not put off? Then also see **Driving**, page 114. There are only a few entry points into Russia by road so check your route with the Embassy before departure.

By boat: it is possible to reach St Petersburg by sea. The Baltic Express Line operates services from Helsinki, Kiel and Stockholm.

A Russian traffic hazard: snow

Business

Moscow is the business capital of Russia and there are centres and conference facilities all over the city, mostly in the large hotels. Facilities in the best of them (see below) offer first-class telecommunications (including satellite), fax, computers, laser printers, photocopying equipment, secretarial assistance, translators and interpreters and other staff who will assist with arranging meetings and organising tours.
In Moscow: Americom Business Center, Radisson Slavjanskaya Hotel, Berezhkovskaya Naberezhnaya 2 (tel: 941 8417, fax: 240 6915); Metropol Business Center, Teatralniy Proezd 1/4 (tel: 927 6000).

Service Globus offers assistance with visas, with organising shows and exhibitions, hotel bookings, hiring chauffeur cars and arranging tickets, translation and sightseeing: Bolshaya Kommunisticheskaya Ulitsa 1–5 (tel: 298 6146, fax: 298 6149).
In St Petersburg: Business Centre, Grand Hotel Europe, Mikhaylovskaya Ulitsa 1/7 (tel: 119 6000, fax: 119 6001) LDM Complex, Professora Popova Ulitsa 47 (tel: 234 4494, fax: 234 9818). Anyone doing business in Russia might be glad of the *Russia Survival Guide* – contact Russian Information Services, Bolshaya Kondradtevskiy Pereulok 4 (tel: 254 9275); or *St Petersburg Business Guide*, Bolshaya Morskaya Ulitsa 20 (tel: 314 5982, fax: 315 3592).

DIRECTORY

Camping

Site places must be booked in advance. When you have done this and paid for your trip you will be issued with a 'camping pass', which confirms the booking and which must be included with your visa application.

Moscow's two camping sites are Mozhaiskaya at 165 Mozhaiskoe Shosse, approximately 10 miles (16km) west of the city (tel: 446 1754; Metro: Kuntsevskaya); open 1 June to 1 September, and Butovo at Bolshaya Butovskaya Ulitsa 5 (tel: 548 7450; Metro: Yuzhnaya, then bus 735). St Petersburg's sites are Olgino

The cold has its compensations for Russia's younger generation

Hotel Camping at Primorskoe Shosse, 11 miles (18km) (tel: 238 3552) and Retur Camping (recommended) also on Primorskoe Shosse, 18 miles (29km) (tel: 237 7533). The overnight charge usually includes the cost of electricity, cooking facilities, kitchen utensils and tableware, as well as the use of sanitary and laundry facilities. It is possible to hire camping equipment in Russia but, to be on the safe side, take your own. The same applies to food – take as much as you can with you.

Chemist see Pharmacist

Crime

Anyone reading the newspapers will be aware that Russia is currently experiencing a crime wave, exacerbated by the freeing-off of the Soviet police state. Generally speaking, it's violent crime that makes the news and here tourists can be reassured that they are very rarely the target of Russia's infamous criminal mafia gangs. Generally speaking from the visitors' perspective, Moscow and St Petersburg are no more dangerous than any other major Western city. The following sensible precautions however, should always be observed. Don't carry large quantities of money on your person if you can possibly avoid it. Keep jewellery, watches and cameras out of sight at all times. Carry photocopies of your passport and visa, leaving the originals in your hotel safe. Also keep the numbers of travellers' cheques and credit cards. At night, avoid the poorly-lit side streets and try not to venture out alone. Tourists need not be over-concerned about travelling on the metro at night – it is well staffed and, by Western standards, comparatively safe. Always change money in one of the many currency exchange offices – although people on the street may offer a competitive rate, they may well be fraudsters dealing in counterfeit. You may be confronted at the entrance to a metro station or on the street, by gangs of children or poorly-dressed families. The ostensible motive is begging but never stop to hear the hard luck story – many if not most, of these down-and-outs are potential muggers.

One small, but important, point – jaywalking is taken very seriously in Russia, so always obey the lights, or, in the daytime at least, use underpasses. If you hear a policeman's whistle, on no account ignore it. If you are the victim of any crime, immediately inform your tour representative or someone at the hotel and then your Embassy – most major hotels have their own police section.

Customs Regulations

The present government inherited the stringent, not to say xenophobic Soviet customs regulations many of which are still, technically at least, in place. At the moment the situation is so confused that there is still not even a printed copy of the up-to-date regulations. If you are in any doubt about purchases consult your Embassy or Aeroservice, Sheremetevo-2 (tel: 578 9030, English and German spoken).

Customs Declaration Forms: all foreign currency in travellers' cheques and banknotes, and all valuables (including watches, medals, rings, radios, computers) taken into Russia, must be declared on a Customs Declaration Form. Keep this safe – you will need it to change money and it must be handed over at the airport prior to departure.

Allowances: you can bring any amount of foreign currency into Russia, but not roubles.

DIRECTORY

Duty-free allowances are as for all countries outside the European Union. It is absolutely forbidden to take antiques, icons or works of art out of the country without permission from the Ministry of Culture. There is also a limit to the value of souvenirs and gifts you are supposed to take out, so keep all receipts. Currently all items purchased for roubles, above the values of 300,000 roubles are subject to a 66% export tax, payable in roubles at the airport. Some foreigners have reported instances where customs officers have demanded duty on trivial items (woollen hats for example!). If you encounter difficulties with officials, politeness and a smile may encourage them to be flexible. On departure, you will fill out another declaration form which will be compared with the original form.

Departure/airport tax: this is usually included in the cost of your airline ticket; if in doubt check with your travel agent.

Driving

You will need a translated international driving licence and, to be on the safe side, a national licence. If you intend driving your own car, take out a short-term insurance policy to cover accidents, damage and third-party liability with the Russian insurance organisation, *Ingosstrakh,* Pyatnitskaya Ulitsa 12 (or contact Intourist for details). Ingosstrakh insists on its coverage in many cases. Traffic in Russia travels on the right. The speed limit is 37mph (60kph) in central Moscow and 56mph (90kph) on the outer roads. Traffic coming from the right has right of way. Trams and buses have priority over other vehicles. If a tram stops to pick up passengers, you must wait for it to move off again before overtaking. At traffic lights you cannot turn right on red. Turning left from major roads often involves taking a right turn first, then making a U-turn and heading back across the intersection. Full headlights are not usually used at night. It is compulsory to wear seat belts and be warned: drunk driving is punished very severely – drink NO alcohol when driving in Russia.

Parking: you can park almost anywhere, within reason. The 'No Parking' sign is a blue circle with diagonal red cross. To be on the safe side, park in or in the vicinity of hotels and on main, well-lit streets.

Theft: many Russians moonlight as mechanics and you may well find hub caps, wing mirrors and even whole cars disappearing if you're not careful. Make sure your car is locked at all times.

Accident or breakdown: in case of accident, breakdown, or traffic infringement you will come into contact with the Russian Traffic Police, the GAI. Officers wear a grey or dark blue uniform and use their batons to signal for you to pull over. On-the-spot fines for minor violations are the norm; in more serious cases you will be asked to surrender your driving licence which will be held at the GAI. Unfortunately there are corrupt GAI officers who may invent a reason for stopping you simply in order to extract a fine which they will pocket themselves – there is little defence against this and the best thing you can do is negotiate!

Maps: Information Moscow maps, Leninskiy Prospekt 45, kv 426 (tel: 135 1164) publish separate street atlases, country road books, town maps and a motorists' guide, all in English. Obviously it's paramount to have an up-to-date map as names of streets, metro stations and even towns have changed over the last few years.

Driving conditions: the state of the roads in Russia is uniformly appalling – even the major thoroughfares like Moscow's Garden Ring Road have poor

Entertainment can range from Russian folk songs performed on the balalaika to the best of cosmopolitan culture

surfaces. Add to this problems of language, one-way streets, poor street lighting, inadequate signing and eccentric parking restrictions and you may well feel it's a better bet to hire a car with driver.

Car hire: there are dozens of car hire firms including: in Moscow, Avis Car Rental, Berezhkovskaya Naberezhnaya 12 (tel: 240 9863); Hertz, Prospekt Mira 49/11 (tel: 284 4391) or Intourtrans, Ulitsa Petrovka 15/13 (tel: 929 8773); and in St Petersburg, Avis, Konnogvardeyskiy Bulvar 4 (tel: 312 6318), Autotur, Energetikov Prospekt 65 (tel: 226 9539) or Automobile Rental, Pribaltiyskaya Hotel (tel: 356 9329).
Bearing in mind the cheapness and efficiency of the public transport system in Moscow and St Petersburg however, you may prefer to forget a car altogether.

DIRECTORY

Electricity

The standard current in Russia is 220 volts. For power sockets you will need a plug or an adaptor with circular pins.

Embassies and Consulates

Australia: 13 Kropotkinskiy Pereulok (tel: 956 6070)
Canada: 23 Starokonyushenny Pereulok (tel: 241 1111)
UK: 14 Sofiyskaya Naberezhnaya (tel: 230 6333)
US: 19/23 Novinskiy Bulvar (tel: 252 2451)
The US Consulate-General in St Petersburg is at Ulitsa Furshtadtskaya 15 (tel: 274 8689)
The UK Consulate-General is at Proletarskoy Diktatury Ploshchad 5 (tel: 119 6036)

Emergency Telephone Numbers

Fire 01, police 02, medical assistance 03.

Entertainment Information

Available from Intourist. There is an Intourist desk in every large hotel which caters for foreigners. The *Moscow News*, *Moscow*

Spasskaya Tower in Red Square

Times and *Moscow Tribune* (free of charge in many hotels), *Neva News*, *St Petersburg Press* and *St Petersburg for you*, and (in German) *St Petersburgiche Zeitung* all have listings pages.

Entry Formalities see Arriving

Health Matters
Check with your travel agent before you book your holiday or buy your ticket.
Vaccinations: no immunisations are required. But it is recommended that you are 'in-date' for polio and tetanus (within 10 years) and typhoid fever. Children should also have diptheria injections.
AIDS is on the increase in Russia and the parliament is considering legislation which would demand mandatory testing for HIV of all foreign visitors.
For the latest information, contact MASTA, Keppel Street, London WC1E 7AT (tel: 0171 631 4408).
Health precautions: do not drink the tap water in St Petersburg. Use mineral water to clean your teeth and do not take ice with your drinks.
Medical treatment: the Russian health service is chronically under-funded and should be avoided. Nowadays a range of private medical treatment is available to foreigners, and the Western centres offer ambulance, medical evacuation and pharmaceutical services. The following organisations are recommended: Moscow – American Medical Center, 2-ya Tverskaya-Yamskaya Ulitsa 10 (new phone number not yet

available); Athens Medical Center, Michurinskiy Prospekt 6 (tel: 143 2387). St Petersburg – American Medical Center, Reki Fontanki Naberezhnaya 77 (tel: 119 6101).
Before travelling to Russia, make sure your medical insurance covers evacuation in case of emergency.

Holidays
1 January (New Year's Day)
7 January (Russian Orthodox Christmas)
8 March (International Women's Day)
1–2 May (Spring Holiday)
9 May (Victory (1945) Day)
12 June (Russian Independence Day)
7–8 November (former anniversary of October Revolution)
On public holidays museums and shops (except food shops) are closed.

Lost Property
Lost and found on the Moscow Metro, Universitet Station, floor 2 Korn 58 (tel: 222 2085).
Lost and found on Moscow Public Transport, Nikolskaya Ulitsa 8, Kor 2 (tel: 923 8753). St Petersburg Public Transport Lost Property, Zakharevskaya Ulitsa 19 (tel: 278 3690).

Media
Newspapers: international newspapers and magazines, including the *International Herald Tribune, The Times, The Guardian, Die Welt, Le Monde, Time* and *Newsweek* are available in all major hotels and in some kiosks on the main shopping streets.

DIRECTORY

Several locally-published English-language newspapers are now available and provide useful listings as well as articles on local life. In Moscow they include the dailies *Moscow Times* and *The Moscow Tribune* and the weekly *Moscow News*; in St Petersburg, the *Neva News, Neva Week* and the *St Petersburg Press*. Free copies are often available in hotel lobbies.

Radio and TV: there are two main Russian TV channels, Ostankino 1 and 2 as well as local stations and an education channel. American and European programmes are imported to Russia via cable and satellite. Most of the main hotels offer cable TV with CNN, while Channel 3 broadcasts the CBS evening news at 19.00hrs and also BBC and ITN bulletins dubbed into Russian. Radio Moscow on 64.4 MHz has an English-language service and broadcasts news every hour. Radio 7 on 104.7 FM or 73.4 AM plays rock music and also has English news bulletins on the half-hour. Radio Maximum on 103.7 FM broadcasts pop and rock music interspersed with English-language discussions of cultural events, current affairs etc. The BBC World Service and Voice of America also broadcast to Moscow. In St Petersburg the World Service can be found on 1260 AM.

Money Matters

The Russian unit of currency is the rouble in denominations of 1, 5, 10, 20, 50 and 100. Notes are for 5, 10, 20, 50, 100, 200, 500, 1,000, 5,000, 10,000, 50,000 and 100,000 roubles.

The exchange rate is stated as roubles per dollar and fluctuates wildly.

As of 1 January 1994 transactions in Western currency were officially forbidden although some street traders still ask for payment in dollars. In Russia the dollar is king so bring plenty with you. Never accept torn or damaged notes – even banks are reluctant to accept soiled notes because of the prevalence of counterfeits. Major credit cards are more convenient than carrying cash and are accepted in large restaurants and hotels, even for small purchases. You can also use them to get cash from banks and hotels, but take your passport for identification. Foreign bank offices in Moscow: Barclays, Mamonovskiy Pereulok 4 (tel: 956 3100); National Westminster, Pokrovskiy Bulvar 4/17 (tel: 975 3397); Midland Bank, World Trade Center, Office 1305 (tel: 253 2145); Bank of America, World Trade Center, Office 1605 (tel: 253 7054). American Express: Moscow – Sadovaya-Kudrinskaya Ulitsa 21a (tel 254 4505); St Petersburg – Grand Hotel Europe (tel: 119 6009).

Opening Times

Shops generally open from 09.00 or 10.00 to 20.00 or 21.00hrs, Monday to Saturday, with an hour for lunch. Most food stores also open on Sundays. The **What to See** section gives times for individual museums, but check with your hotel before you set out. Museums generally are open on Sundays. Banks open from 09.00 to 18.00hrs; but many break for lunch.

St Petersburg's Church of St Nicholas

Pharmacist

If you are on medication, make sure you take a full supply of the required drugs/preparations with you, as you are unlikely to obtain them in Russia. You will also need your own supply of contraceptives, tampons or sanitary towels, aspirin and diarrhoea tablets. If you are visiting St Petersburg during the summer months, you will need some form of anti-mosquito repellent. If you have a baby or small child with you, take your own supply of nappies. Bear in mind that none of these everyday items is readily available in Russia. Avoid the standard Russian *apteka* (pharmacy) as these have limited and unreliable supplies of drugs. Use the increasing number of Western-sponsored pharmacies instead (English usually spoken). For example in Moscow – Stariy Arbat Pharmacy, Ulitsa Arbat 25 (tel: 291 7101) or Drugstore at Sadko Arcade (tel: 253 9592); in St Petersburg – Pharmacy Damian, Moskovskiy Prospekt 22 (tel 110 1744) and PetroFarm, Nevskiy Prospekt 22 (tel: 314 5401) (closed Saturday).

DIRECTORY

Places of Worship

Moscow
Orthodox: Church of the Resurrection, Brusov Pereulok 15 (Metro: Okhotniy Ryad).
St Nicholas in Khamovnikakh (the Weavers' Church), Lva Tolstogo Ulitsa 2 (Metro: Park Kultury).
Holy Trinity, Universitetskaya Ploshchad 1 (Metro: Kievskaya).

Baptist: Malyy Trekhsvyatitelskiy Pereulok 3 (Metro: Chistye Prudy).
Mosque: Vypolzov Pereulok 7 (Metro: Prospekt Mira).
Protestant: St Andrew Anglican Church, Voznesenskiy Pereulok 8 (Metro: Okhotniy Ryad).
Roman Catholic: St Louis, Lubyanka Malaya Ulitsa 12 (Metro: Lubyanka).

The St Petersburg Metro

Synagogue: Bolshaya Spasoglinishchevskiy Pereulok 8 (Metro: Chistye Prudy).

St Petersburg
Orthodox: St Nicholas, Ploshchad Nikolskaya 1. Trinity Cathedral, Reki Monastyrki Naberezhnaya 1 (Metro: Ploshchad Aleksandra Nevskogo)
Baptist: Bolshaya Ozornaya Ulitsa 29a
Mosque: Kronverkskiy Prospekt 7 (Metro: Gorkovskaya)
Roman Catholic: Kovenskiy Pereulok 7 (Metro: Ploshchad Vosstaniya)
Synagogue: Lermontovskiy Prospekt 2

Police

The emergency police telephone number is 02. See also **Crime**, page 112.

Post Office

Every major hotel has its own post office counter where you can buy postcards, stamps and envelopes (newspaper kiosks also sell stamps). There will also be a post box in your hotel and you can send telegrams from here. Packages must be wrapped at post offices.

Moscow: the main Post Office is at Myasnitskaya Ulitsa 26/2 (tel: 924 0250); open from 08.00 to 19.45hrs.
The Central Telegraph Office is located at Tverskaya Ulitsa 7 (24-hour service; tel: 924 9004). International telephone calls can also be made from here.
St Petersburg: Central Post Office, Pochtantskaya 9 (tel: 312 8305); open 09.00 to 21.00hrs.

Central Telegraph Office, Pochtantskaya Ulitsa 15 (24-hour service).
Post boxes are blue and white. Outbound mail can take three weeks but is generally reliable.

Public Transport

Metro: Moscow and St Petersburg both have cheap, clean, safe and efficient Metro systems and you will certainly want to use them. However, a basic knowledge of the cyrillic alphabet is indispensable if you are to avoid getting lost, so it is worth investing some time to master it before you embark on your holiday (see **Language**, page 125).
Before you set out, note down the cyrillic form of the station you are heading for, together with the names of any stations where you have to change lines. If you get lost you can ask someone to help you of course, but this is not easy during the rush hours. You will be less likely to panic if you have a friend with you, so avoid travelling alone if possible. Stations are indicated by a large red neon letter **M**. There is a flat fare irrespective of the distance you are travelling or the number of changes you intend to make. You pay again only if you break your journey by passing through the exit barrier. Payment is by token (*talon*) obtainable from ticket windows in the station foyer. These tokens are also valid on other forms of transport. The escalators are usually deep (especially in St Petersburg) so if you suffer from vertigo, hold on tight to the handrail! Once you arrive on the platform you can

DIRECTORY

expect a train within five minutes, even outside the rush hours.

You will usually be able to find a seat on the train, but if you are young and able-bodied, be prepared to stand for an elderly person (simply point to your seat and say *Pazhalsta*). As the train pulls into the next station its name will be announced, followed by any information about changing lines. So if you listen carefully and keep an eye on the map, you will be able to check whether you are going in the right direction or not. Changing lines takes time and can be tricky. To know which direction to go in, look for a sign with the word *perekhold* (переход) and the name of the station you want. To get to street level, look for the sign *vykhod* (выход).

Basic signs:

entrance вход
exit выход
no entry нет входа
cash desk касса
to trains for stations… к поездам до станчий
change trains for stations… переход на поезда до станчий
exit for the town выход в город
to the exit к выходу

The Metros of both cities open from 06.00 to 01.00hrs sharp.

Buses, trams and trolleybuses: trams are commonplace in St Petersburg but not so common nowadays in Moscow. You will find buses and trolleybuses in both cities. All these forms of transport tend to be rather uncomfortable and crowded but you might like to take a ride just for the experience. Fares are the same as for the Metro. Either buy your ticket from the driver or get on with your tokens (*talony*) obtainable from kiosks or from the Metro. Drop your coins into the box near the driver or at the back of the vehicle. If you can not get through, pass your token to a neighbour and say *Piridayite, pazhalsta* ('Pass it on please'). You will eventually be given a white paper ticket in return.

Taxis: you can ask your hotel desk to book a taxi for you, but make sure you order it at least an hour in advance. The city cabs are yellow, with a chequered band on the sides or roof. A taxi stand is marked with the letter **T**. A green light in the corner of the windscreen indicates that a taxi is for hire. For security reasons it is advisable to use hotel taxis. Private taxis are available in abundance but bear in mind that there is no guarantee that all drivers are fully insured, nor that all vehicles are roadworthy. In any case never travel in a cab when there is already someone inside and always negotiate the fare in advance because only official taxis have meters.

Central Moscow Taxi Bureau: Novaya Ploshchad 8/10 (tel: 927 0000); 24-hr service.

St Petersburg, Astoria-Service, Borovaya Ulitsa 11/13 (tel: 164 9622).

Student and Youth Travel

Youth exchanges are organised by Moskovskiy Sputnik, Malay Ivanovskiy Pereulok 6, kor 2 (tel: 925 9278) and St Petersburg Sputnik, Chapygina Ulitsa 4 (tel: 234 0249).

You may prefer to use the hotel phone, rather than queue for a booth

Accommodation: Sputnik Hotel (Moscow), Leninskiy Prospekt 38 (tel: 938 7057); Traveller's Guest House Moscow (affiliate of International Youth Hostelling Association), Bolshaya Pereyaslavskaya Ulitsa 50, floor 10 (tel: 971 4059).
Russian Youth Hostel (St Petersburg – also affiliate of IYHA), 3-ya Sovetskaya Ulitsa 28 (tel: 277 0569).

Telephones
The Moscow area code is 095. The St Petersburg area code is 812. Telephone boxes for calls within Russia can be found all over the city. For international calls, faxes and telexes go to your hotel reception desk or business centre or a main post office. For information on international calling in Moscow dial 8-190 and ask for an English-speaking operator. In St Petersburg the same service is available on 315 0012. The pocket-sized *Traveller's Yellow Pages* and *Handbook for Moscow*, published by InfoServices International, inc, New York, USA, contains more than 8,000 useful phone numbers as well as a wide variety of other information, plans etc. A similar guide is available for St Petersburg.

Time
Moscow and St Petersburg are three hours ahead of London and eight hours ahead of Washington and New York; seven hours behind Sydney; and nine hours behind New Zealand. Summer time (when local time is one hour in advance of the rest of the year) is from April until the end of September.

Tipping
Officially it does not exist but actually tips are expected from Western tourists in certain

DIRECTORY

situations. In restaurants leave a small tip in dollars only if merited (service and other charges are always included). Taxi drivers too will appreciate a small tip in dollars. Hotel staff, such as the maid and the *dezhurnaya*, will welcome a small gift of perfume, talcum powder or cigarettes.

Toilets

Russian public toilets are noxious, unpleasant and unhygenic, so use the facilities in hotels as far as possible. Even the toilets in major museums fall well below Western standards. If you do need to use a public convenience you will need your own supply of toilet paper or tissues. There are the most primitive conveniences at main line stations and at many of the major tourist attractions. The nearest public toilet to Red Square is in GUM or by the Kutafya Tower. There are several pay toilets on Nevskiy Prospekt in St Petersburg – numbers 20, 39 and 50.

Tourist Offices

The travel monopoly of Intourist has now been broken although the firm is still a major operator.

Intourist

Moscow: Mokhovaya Ulitsa 13 (tel: 292 2037)
Canada: 1801 McGill College Avenue, Montreal, Quebec
UK: Intourist House, Meridian Gate, Marsh Wall, London E14
US: 630 5th Avenue, Suite 868, New York, NY 10111.

A St Petersburg ice cream stall

LANGUAGE

A few hours spent mastering the Russian alphabet before you go will be amply rewarded. Being able to decipher street names, metro stations, etc, will give you the freedom to wander around by yourself, rather than being shepherded in a group.

The interior of the dome of St Isaac's Cathedral in St Petersburg

Useful words and phrases

hello	zdrávstvuytye	здравствуйте
goodbye	dasvidániya	до свидания
good morning	dóbraya útra	доброе утро
good evening	dóbry viécher	добрый вечер
good night	spakóyni nóchi	спокойной ночи
please/you're welcome	pazhálsta	пожалуйста
thank you	spasíba	спасибо
yes	da	да
no	niét	нет
excuse me	izvinítye	извините
where?	gdyé?	где?
when?	kagdá?	когда?
how many?	skólka?	сколько?
how much?	skólka?	сколько?
I	ya	Я
we	my	мы
left	naliéva	налево
right	napráva	направо
straight on	pryáma	прямо
I don't speak Russian	ya nye gavaryú pa-rússki	Я не говорю по-русски
can you speak English?	vy gavarítye pa-anglíyski?	Вы говорите по-англцйски?
write down please	napishíte eta, pazhálsta	Напишите это, пожалуйста

LANGUAGE

Alphabet

А	ah
Б	b
В	v
Г	g
Д	d
Е	ye (yellow)
Ё	yaw
Ж	zh
З	z
И	ee
Й	i (boil)
К	k
Л	l
М	m
Н	n
О	o (not)
П	o
Р	r
С	s
Т	t
У	ooh
Ф	f
Х	ch (Loch)
Ц	ts
Ч	ch (chain)
Ш	sh
Щ	shch (Ashchurch)
Ъ	hard sign
Ы	i (sin)
Ь	soft sign
Э	ay
Ю	yooh
Я	yah

Signs

entrance	вход
exit	выход
no entrance	нет входа
free entrance	вход свободный
toilet	туалет
gentlemen	мужской
ladies	женский
stop	стой, стойте
go	идите
crossing	переход
closed	закрыто
open	открыто
cash desk	касса
reserved, occupied	занято
vacant	свободно
no smoking	нельзя курить!
push	толкайте
pull	тяните
information	справочное бюро
restaurant	ресторан
lift	лифт
telephone	телефон
taxi	такси
street	улица
buffet	буфет
bar	бар
museum	музей
theatre	театр
books	книги
record shop (Melodiya)	мелодия
chemist	Аптека

INDEX/ACKNOWLEDGEMENTS

Acknowledements

The Automobile Association would like to thank the following photographers and
libraries for their assistance in the preparation of this book:

AA PHOTO LIBRARY 41, 87, 92 (J Arnold), 23, 35, 91, 97, 109 (K Paterson)

J ALLAN CASH PHOTO LIBRARY 9 Moskva River, 16 University, 38 Tsar Cannon, 50 Tomb
of Peter the Great, 56 Hermitage, 59 Winter Palace, 93 Cosmos Hotel, 96 Ukrain Hotel, 98
Mariinskiy Theatre, 111 Petrol Station.

P CORY 31 Alexander Gardens.

NATURE PHOTOGRAPHERS LTD 75 Hooded Crow (A J Cleave), 77 Saiga Antelope 78
Taiga (B Burbidge), 81 European Bison (S C Bisserot).

ELLEN ROONEY Cover: Novodevichiy Convent, Smolensk Cathedral, Moscow

SPECTRUM COLOUR LIBRARY 6 Buskers Arbat Street, 10 Kremlin, 13 Cathedral of the
Dormition, 18 Underground, 32 Shop Windows, 55 Aurora, 65 Alexander Nevskiy
Monastery, 72 Smolniy Convent, 84 Food & Drink Kiosk, 89 Russian Dolls, 94 Rossiya Hotel,
105 Souvenirs, 106 Harbour Ferry, 123 Telephone Booths, 124 Ice Cream Seller.

ZEFA PICTURE LIBRARY UK LTD 4 Moscow at night, 15 St Nicholas Church, 26/7
Novodevichiy Convent, 45 Historical Museum, 48 Sergievo Posad's Cathedral of
Assumption, 49 Peter I, 52 Palace Square, 53 Senate Square, 62 Peter-Paul Fortress, 69
Nevskiy Prospekt, 74 Peterhof Palace, 101 Sergievo Posad, 103 River Moika, 116
Spasskaya Tower, 119 St Nicholas Church, 120 Pushkin Station.

RUSSIA & REPUBLICS PHOTO LIBRARY 20 Pushkin Museum of Fine Art, 28 Museum of Serf
Art, 66 Pushkin, 83 Farmer's Market, 112 Mother & Child, 115 Balalaika Player, 126 St
Isaacs'.

Contributors:
Thanks to **Christopher** and **Melanie Rice** for their detailed revision work